Praise for *Magic of NLP Demystified Second Edition*

Byron Lewis has offered another fine texture to the tapestry that is NLP through his book *Magic of NLP Demystified*, Second Edition. This book is a very rich and deep presentation of the most important building blocks in Neuro Linguistic Programming and the relationship to Psychology. In fact if you don't understand in depth these patterns then you don't know NLP. This book will very much enhance the map of NLP in the field.

Judith Delozier, Author and co-developer of NLP

My original copy of *Magic of NLP Demystified* is threadbare. Well thumbed and coffee stained it was an invaluable early guide to NLP for me. Now in 2012 I'm delighted that Byron Lewis has revisited the territory. The new distinctions they make offer new insights. I'm going to be returning to this new text many times too. Simple to read but not simplistic Lewis provides an easy way in to the magic of language and change.

Ian McDermott, Founder, International Teaching Seminars

I have been using *Magic of NLP Demystified* as per study for my NLP Certification programmes since 1995. ple to read introduction to some of the models that Neuro Linguistic Programm re an entrepreneur, teacher, manager, sal omeone who wants to communicate mor able you to unlock some of the magic tha

David Shephard, Certified Master Trainer Of NLP, President of The American Board Of NLP, Co-Author of *Presenting Magically*

Whether you've just fallen in love with NLP or you are an old-timer who was trained many years ago, you'll find great value in *Magic of NLP Demystified* - as a newcomer you will be enriched by material fundamental to NLP and you'll discover the roots from which many current techniques have grown. More experienced practitioners will gain from a thorough review of the h inks to the latest discoveries adable and experiential bo g and teaching

NLP can bring. This second edition of the *Magic of NLP Demystified* is a must for every serious student of NLP.

James Lawley and Penny Tompkins, Authors of *Metaphors in Mind: Transformation through Symbolic Modelling*

The new edition of *Magic of NLP Demystified* is an excellent book that anyone committed to becoming a professional communicator needs to have. It deals with the very heart of NLP – the language model that makes up the very best Communication Model that anyone has yet to come up with. I'm grateful for the addition to the additional Meta-Model distinctions that I contributed. Byron Lewis has created an excellent update of their foundational work!

L. Michael Hall, Ph.D.

The Magic of

NLP

Demystified

Byron Lewis

Crown House Publishing Limited
www.crownhouse.co.uk
www.crownhousepublishing.com

First published by

Crown House Publishing Ltd
Crown Buildings, Bancyfelin, Carmarthen, Wales, SA33 5ND, UK
www.crownhouse.co.uk

and

Crown House Publishing Company LLC
6 Trowbridge Drive, Suite 5, Bethel, CT 06801, USA
www.crownhousepublishing.com

Cover design www.sixteen-design.co.uk. Cover image © Lom - Fotolia.com

First published in paperback by Metamorphous Press (ISBN 1555520170)

British Library of Cataloguing-in-Publication Data
A catalogue entry for this book is available from the British Library.

Print ISBN 978-184590803-4
Mobi ISBN 978-184590817-1
ePub ISBN 978-184590818-0

LCCN 2011940615

Printed and bound in the UK by
Bell & Bain Ltd, Glasgow

Foreword

This work represents the culmination of several years of training and self-exploration within the confines of a specific sphere of study. It was in the early 1970s that I was led through a powerful therapeutic experience by two important people in my life, Frank Pucelik and Leslie Cameron (now Lebeau). That session had a profound and lasting effect on me. Soon after the experience I found myself thinking, "I want to learn how to do that kind of magic!" And so I did.

With the help of Leslie and Frank, I became a member of a small experimental-research therapy group in Santa Cruz, California. Thus I became one of a growing number of people who were actually studying the *magic* of therapeutic growth and change. This extremely creative and generative group centered around two exciting and charismatic individuals: Richard Bandler and John Grinder. Caught up in the enthusiastic energy of the group, I found my perceptions heightening, my abilities growing, and my own model of the world expanding as if by magic.

It wasn't enough, however, to simply learn how to do this therapeutic wizardry. I wanted to share it with others. I began to compile notebooks detailing my learning experiences which included the outline and notes from Frank's comprehensive Meta training that formed the basis for this book. In addition I started to see clients under the supervision of therapists who were also interested in the Meta materials. It didn't take long to develop a style of my own, and I labeled my notes "A Model for a Process Theory of Personality." I was sure I had found "the right track." It took a while for me to become aware of the trap I had set for myself.

As I read and continued to study and work with people, I discovered that my model was continually being stretched, extended, expanded, and enlarged. But just as often it was also shrunk, crushed, pierced, and mutilated. I was amazed. It was during a moment of quiet desperation that I created a symbolic representation of the wonderful contradictions confronting me. It represented both the confusion I was feeling (don't get me wrong – I thoroughly enjoyed it!) and recognition of the trap from which I was escaping, the trap of thinking that there is only one reliable, accurate, and successful path to therapeutic growth and change. The symbol held an important place tacked to the wall above my typewriter. It looked like this:

While the goal of this book is to present models of basic Meta principles that underlie the "magic" of effective change-oriented communication, it is essential to keep in mind how important it is to remain open to experience in order to prevent becoming trapped or limited by a model. Towards that end, the text provides regular reminders that emphasize that there are always alternatives. We need only learn how to recognize them.

December 27, 1979
Byron A. Lewis

Preface

It has been over thirty years since I penned the words in the Foreword to the original *Magic Demystified: A Pragmatic Guide to Communication and Change*. It astounds me that after all these years, the book continues to be read, continues to be sold and traded, and used by individuals all over the world. It has even been translated into a number of different languages. And it is now to be reborn through the efforts of our friends at Crown House Publishing.*

In that time, a great deal of attention has been focused on Neuro-Linguistic Programming (NLP), and not all of it has been positive. Some have justifiably complained that observations of a few of the early writers in the field did not stand up to the scrutiny of rigorous scientific research. Others have been critical of the more flamboyant claims – especially of some of the earlier writers and practitioners – as to exactly what NLP can do.[1] It is my hope that in revising this work, we can direct readers to some of the research that has been done over the last few decades as well as the numerous writings showing the depth and breadth of applications of NLP. Like Tosey and Mathison (2009), I want this book to reflect and support "an approach to NLP that is enquiring, research-based and critical" (p. 4).

The formation of organizations such as the Association for NLP[2] and the NLP Research Conferences[3] that started just a few years ago are very exciting developments for the growing field of inquiry into NLP. As an example, the call for papers for the 2012 NLP Research Conference includes a request for "empirical research into the application of NLP to people development and change, across fields such as business and management, coaching, education, health and psychotherapy," among other topics.[4] Another popular forum for exchange of innovative ideas and research in NLP, the Institute for the Advanced Studies of Health, in their call for proposals for their 2012 World Health Conference, asks for "presentations or workshops supporting the theme 'Emerging Fields of NLP: Modeling NLP for the Future.'"

For those new to the field, it is important to understand the fact that NLP was not created in a vacuum or formed without research. Tosey and Mathison (2009) go so far as to state: "there is a case for saying that the development of the meta-model, indeed the groundwork behind much of NLP in the 1970s, was strongly research-based. Bandler and Grinder engaged in a form of empirical research through observation, analysis, experimentation and continuous testing" (p. 52).

I was fortunate to have been part of that early research. As an undergraduate student at University of California, Santa Cruz when Richard and John were writing their premier works *The Structure of Magic, Vol. I* and *Vol. II*, I was occasionally called to join them at their home on Alba Road to "work" with someone. Once there, I was provided with an outline of what had been done and instructions for continuing the process. I was to "report back" on what was working and what wasn't as I interacted with the individual over the next hour or so. This would go on until one of them was convinced the "client" had accomplished what he or she had asked for, and they had "tested" the results to confirm that change had occurred.

I had always thought I was being invited simply because of my student status. While this was true, it wasn't the only reason. It was much later that I discovered they were actually conducting a form of research to test the patterns they had observed being used by therapists such as Virginia Satir, Fritz Perls, and Milton Erickson. However, they were concerned that their own unconscious use "of non-verbal patterns of influence with our clients constituted an obstacle to sorting out the impact of the verbal patterns we were modeling. We were inadvertently influencing our clients in ways that were confounding the research we were engaged in. The three of us (Bandler, Pucelik, and Grinder) attempted to eliminate such variables in order to appreciate solely the effects of the set of verbal patterns we were testing" (Bostic St. Clair and Grinder, 2001, p. 148).

The above authors go on to describe how, in order to address this issue, they would send in "one or more of our students into the room, well rehearsed and strictly instructed to limit their interactions with the client to the set of verbal patterns we were exploring and then to report back to us the results of the work. They would then be instructed by us to return and execute some intervention we determined to be relevant" (p. 148). I was in essence part of a "blind test" experimental procedure!

Another aspect of their early work that in retrospect was very important to me was that the founders and early developers of NLP, including Richard,

John, and Frank, all had huge personalities. I agree with the observation made by Terrence McClendon in his book *The Wild Days: NLP 1972–1981* that "NLP is as much an attitude as anything else" (p. 12). Their enthusiasm and apparent lack of fear to try new things, especially in those early days, gave me the confidence to take chances, try different approaches, and push out my own limits and boundaries, keeping what worked and discarding what didn't. This was a significant change from my earlier experience of "psychology."

My father was a Jungian psychologist, and many of my early memories are of my father's references to one or another of Jung's themes during family discussions. It was not unusual for him to actually pull out one of Jung's books and read aloud a passage to emphasize a point he was trying to make. Even the priests in the church we went to were often Jungian psychologists as well as theologians, and their sermons were generously peppered with references to Jungian archetypes such as the *persona*, the *anima* and *animas*, and the *shadow*. I came to NLP already primed with an appreciation of the importance of the "unconscious mind!" However, as young adult, I also remember hearing my mother recounting her experience of psychoanalysis: "After 14 years of psychoanalytic therapy," she said, "I could tell you *why* I had my problems, but not *what to do* about them!"[5]

This may explain in part my early attraction to NLP. My profound encounter with Frank's almost "magical" use of language to invoke the imagery, feelings, and voices in my head, and to orchestrate the experience in such a way that I was able to break self-imposed boundaries that were defeating my ability to "move on" with my life, had nothing whatsoever to do with any intellectual "understanding" of my problems. The experience simply worked to help me shift ways of thinking and responding that were less effective in achieving what I wanted. I used to wonder what this approach to "therapy" might have done for my mother. This book is the result of another question Frank and I both had: How else can we share this *magic* with others?

I hope those readers who are new to NLP enjoy this basic introduction to the field. For readers who are taking a second look at this work, I hope you find that it stimulates as many questions as answers and inspires you to continue your own research in the field!

Byron Lewis
December 27, 2011

A PRAGMATIC GUIDE TO COMMUNICATION AND CHANGE

Notes to the Preface

* This revised edition is the first that actually involved the authors. Previous "revised" editions were created by the previous publisher without any input whatsoever from me or Frank, and as far as we can tell, the only actual revision made was to the title which now includes the words "of NLP" after Magic.

1. I visit this problem in my second book *Sobriety Demystified*. In my discussion of "the estrangement of NLP" from mainstream psychology, I observe: "Marilyn Darling (1988), who studied NLP during its formative years, noted that many NLPers tended to overstate their case when describing the applications of NLP. She writes, 'They have made bold and unsubstantiated claims – phobia cures in 10 minutes, lifelong perfect pitch, etc. And they repeat mythic tales of power and wonder' (p. 38). In her article written in defense of NLP, Darling points out that NLP simply hasn't lived up to many of its claims" (Lewis, 1996, p. xvi). However, this may be because NLP, like many of the rapid therapies developed during the same era, does not lend itself well to empirical research, although Tosey and Mathison (2007) acknowledge: "What it does have is accumulated case evidence that has been reviewed over many years through critical dialogue" (p. 139).

2. See http://www.anlp.org.

3. See http://nlpresearchconference.squarespace.com.

4. The call for papers at (http://nlpresearchconference.square-space.com/call-for-papers includes the following guidelines for contributions:

- Empirical research into the application of NLP to people development and change, across fields such as business and management, coaching, education, health, and psychotherapy.

- Practice-based research, including pilot studies and case studies, exploring the use and impact of NLP in a practice setting.

- Critical evaluations and scholarly appraisals of NLP, including historical, social, and cultural perspectives, and including perspectives that challenge the field.

- Advances in the theoretical underpinnings of NLP, including contributions that illuminate the relationship between NLP and contemporary thinking and research in cognate fields (such as cognitive linguistics and neuroscience).

- Evidenced applications of NLP as a research methodology.

5. To underscore this point, Tosey and Mathison (2007) state: "In common with the aspirations of the human potential movement, NLP takes issue with the archaeological emphasis of Freudians, on digging into the past in order to understand the present. NLP is firmly constructivist in the sense that it perceives all experience, including memories, as (re)created in the present" (p. 5).

Acknowledgments

Gratitude is expressed to the following individuals: to Leslie Cameron (now Lebeau) who showed me the path, to Richard Bandler who led me down it, to John Grinder who illuminated it for me, and to Frank Pucelik who set me back on course (repeatedly) and whose immeasurable input into this volume warranted his co-authorship.

Special thanks go to Ron Hill, Ph.D., Nancy Skolnik, Ph.D., and Linnaea Marvell-Mell, whose editing and helpful suggestions were so instrumental in putting the book into its final form, to Marcia Lewis, my wife, for her support and her illustration on page 147, and to Leslie (Antos) Lewis, my sister, for her beautiful and creative illustrations.

Finally, a special thank you to Carol Martin whose well-crafted drawing provided the basis for the the diagram of the 4-tuple and the processes that add social and individual constraints to our models of the world shown in the three illustrations in Chapter 1 and in Appendix A who has gone unrecognized until this second edition.

Contents

Introduction

[W]e must learn to understand the "out-of-awareness" aspects of communication. We must never assume that we are fully aware of what we communicate to someone else. There exists in the world today tremendous distortions in meaning as men try to communicate with one another.

Edward T. Hall, *The Silent Language*

In his book *Persuasion and Healing*, Jerome Frank identified the major goals of various approaches to psychotherapy. These include efforts to reduce the client's distress, increase his self-esteem, help him to function better at work and in his relationships, and "heighten his sense of control over himself and his environment" (p. 200). It is important to note that, as we become aware of some of those "out-of-awareness" aspects of communication referred to by Edward Hall, we enhance the sense of control that Frank has identified as a major goal of psychotherapy. This book is dedicated to improving our ability to perceive, identify, and utilize certain aspects of the communicative process that are not normally in our conscious awareness.

This is also a book about change. It is a collection of effective tools for assisting in the resolution of problems found in many settings. The patterns discussed can assist anyone to more fully participate in and control the growth experience of positive change.

The Meta principles[1] presented in this book encompass many schools of psychological thought. They include elements from each of the following areas of psychology: *behavioral psychology*, which emphasizes observable behavior and stimulus–response connections; *humanistic psychology*, which stresses free will and subjective experience; *cognitive theory*, which covers the transformation of sensory stimulation in terms of coding, storing in memory, and retrieval systems; *traditional psychotherapy*, which deals with conscious and unconscious distinctions of thoughts, fears, and wishes that may or may not manifest themselves in awareness; and information drawn from various neurological studies, especially studies of changes that occur in the nervous system. The term "meta" is used because the model that is developed is *about* rather than *a part* of all of these, and the emphasis is on the processes of change.

This book does not propose a new approach to psychotherapy, a new "philosophy of life," or a new way to get "it." What it does offer is the opportunity to experience personality and communication as *processes*. The text presents a blend of research, theory, and relevant portions of transcripts from therapeutic sessions and educational seminars. The emphasis is on models, for it is through them that we can share a wide range of complex experiences. The medium of study is the process of communication, and special attention is paid to areas generally thought to be unconscious or unaware communicative behavior.

It has been our experience that, with the help of a teacher, counselor, or therapist, people are able to resolve many of their problems. There is often a certain degree of change in personality as a result of insight gained or behavioral modifications programmed into the individual during the sessions. This change assists the individual in "coping" with particular difficulties. What these therapeutic experiences usually do not do, however, is systematically create a *reference structure* – a set of experiences – that would enable a person to change his coping patterns in response to *new* difficulties. In our work with people, we have found that by presenting information to them in specific ways, that is, by being explicit about the *processes* involved in change and positive growth, clients can learn to have many of the same resources the teacher and therapist have for solving problems. This systematic *demystification* of normally out-of-awareness aspects of communication gives the client a heightened sense of control over himself and his environment.[2] Although this is not true for every client, the patterns used to obtain the information about a client's communicative behavior remain the same. Various ways of utilizing this information are presented in the text.

Throughout the book, a variety of techniques are provided as pragmatic applications of the material. They also draw the reader's attention to the processes involved in personality development and maintenance. Use of these processes may assist you in helping those you work and live with to discover more choices about how they perceive the world and themselves and what they might do to lead more comfortable and productive lives. The methods covered in this book may be learned quite rapidly. They are not meant, however, to take the place of any currently in-use psychotherapeutic methodologies. They are offered as an adjunct to existing techniques and as a perceptual paradigm for the serious student of human behavior, communication, and personality.

Throughout we interchange the terms "model of the world," "map," and "model of reality." They all stand for the same concept in this book.[3] There are also places where we have shortened the term "representational system" to simply "system." In these cases, the meaning of the word will be obvious from its context.

With some practice, you may soon find many of the techniques and the perceptual acuity presented here coming into use in your everyday patterns of communication as well as in the professional setting. We invite you to use this book as an opportunity to explore the variables of both internal communication processes and the behavior called "communication" that we experience continuously as social beings.

Notes to the Introduction

1.   At the time this book was originally published, there was some confusion regarding the use of the term Neuro-Linguistic Programming (NLP). Because of the threat (real or imagined) of legal action for "unauthorized" use of the term NLP, we decided to refrain from using it and settled on Meta principles instead. These Meta principles are not to be confused with the presuppositions identified by Wolfgang Walker, as translated and outlined by Tosey and Mathison (2009). We strongly recommend the reader see their very comprehensive discussion of these presuppositions and their roots in cybernetics in that book.

2.   In support of this approach, a working description of NLP offered by Dilts and DeLozier (2000): Defined as *the study of the structure of subjective experience*, NLP studies the patterns or "programming" created by the interaction between the brain ("neuro"), language ("linguistics") and the body. From the NLP perspective, it is this interaction that produces both effective and ineffective behavior, and is responsible for the processes behind both human excellence and pathology (p. 849 original emphasis).

3. Tosey and Mathison (2009) present a very enlightening discussion of representationalism: the notion that our internal experiences are mere representations of some external "reality." They suggest the map vs. model discussions found in many early NLP writings likely originated with Gregory Bateson. They also expand upon the original concept and suggest ultimately that, while the concept of internal representations in NLP is not representationalism, such views "continue to appear, epitomized by the NLP 'communication model'" (p. 69).

Chapter 1
Models

The purpose of the model is to enable the user to do a better job in handling the enormous complexities of life. By using models, we see and test how things work and can even predict how things will go in the future.

Edward T. Hall, *Beyond Culture*

The Use of Models

No other creature we know of is quite as infatuated with the construction and use of models as we humans appear to be. As Hall points out, "We are the model-making organism par excellence" (1976, p. 13). We use these models to represent almost all aspects of our environment, our social organizations, our technology, and even our very life processes. Models of machines, buildings, or bridges help us see and evaluate design and structure. Models of government enable us to understand complex systems of human social behavior. Scientific models assist us in perceiving relationships and properties of theoretical problems and processes.

It is our goal that the psychological and behavioral models presented in this book will operate as Hall suggests. That is, they will reduce the complexities of human communication into a more easily perceived and understandable framework, ultimately enabling you to direct yourself and others toward a healthy and positive future.

Neurological Basis

Our romance with constructing models of our experience of the world may have a basis in psychobiological processes. We cannot escape the limitations imposed by our biological origins.

As Carl Jung observed:

> Man ... never perceives anything fully or comprehends anything com-
> pletely. He can see, hear, touch, taste; but how far he sees, how well he
> hears, what his touch tells him, and what he tastes depend upon the
> number and quality of his senses. ... No matter what instruments he uses,
> at some point he reaches the edge of certainty beyond which conscious
> knowledge cannot pass. (1964, p. 21)

In our constant attempts to understand, driven by some intrinsic need
to explore and explain, we create our models. But we are inexorably separated from the world outside ourselves.[1] Neural transmission, the basis of
what we call perception, is a bioelectric phenomenon. Billions of neurons
make up the human nervous system. Even though sensory input varies
from pressure to temperature to sound to electromagnetic waves, they
are all ultimately transformed into electrochemical impulses as they are
transmitted to the central nervous system. The study of this miraculous
transmutation of energy leads us to a fundamental aspect of experience:
we do not perceive *reality*, but rather a neurological *model* of reality. This is
what forms the basis for what we call our *model of the world*.[2]

The Nerve Cell

The nerve cell represents the first step in the creation of our models of the
world. The basic units of the nerve cell are shown below.

1.   *Cell body* containing nucleus.

2.   *Dendrites*. These extend from the cell body and form the "receiving
     area" for stimulation from outside the body and from other adjacent
     cells.

3.   *Axon*. This single fiber transmits the bioelectric impulse to the axon
     terminal.

4.   *Axon terminal*. This is the part of the nerve cell that activates other
     neurons on the way to or from the central nervous system as well
     as within it. Neural "messages" are also transmitted to muscles and
     glands through the axon terminal.

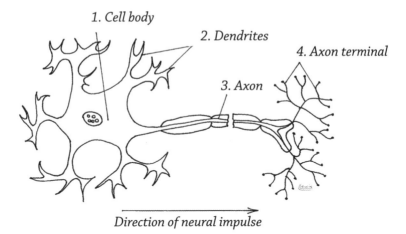

1. Cell body

2. Dendrites

4. Axon terminal

3. Axon

Direction of neural impulse

Because sensory organs vary greatly from one individual to another, each one of us perceives the world differently. These differences may be subtle or great. But since our perceptions form the basis for our models of the world, we must assume that every individual will have a *different* model.

The Reality Model

Due to similarities in neurological mechanisms in each of us, we are able to have similar experiences. These, combined with shared social and cultural experiences, enable the creation of what might be called "consensus realities." These are shared models that form the basis of our social structures. Language is the prime example of such a model. However, it is a fact that there can be no universally shared and accepted representation of experience, no one model of the world that is accurate for everyone, that accounts for the marvelous diversity found in the human personality.

Perceptions Can Be Deceiving

There was an interesting exhibit at the Exploratorium in San Francisco. Two half-inch copper tubes are wound side-by-side around a wooden dowel. Warm fluid is piped through one tube, while cold fluid flows through the other. It was quite a shock to touch or grasp the bundle: the simultaneous sensations of warmth and cold produce a *perceived* extremely hot or burning sensation. It was fun to watch disbelieving people jump after reading the description and then, thinking they will be able to discern the difference, take a firm grasp of the bundle!

Patterns of Rule-Governed Behavior

Although it is important to appreciate the individual nature of perceived reality, it is equally important to identify *patterns* of behavior exhibited by individuals and groups. The observation of these patterns forms the central theme of this work. In his book, *The Silent Language*, Edward Hall states that, "The goal of the investigator who deals with human phenomena is to discover the patterns ... that exist hidden in the minds, the sensory apparatus, and the muscles of man" (p. 115). These bits and pieces of observable behavior go into the making of the process-oriented model of personality presented in this book.

During interactions involved in communication, certain consistencies of behavior become evident. Just as the language we use is structured by semantics and grammar, so does the rich and varied non-linguistic behavior of humans appear to follow a highly structured order. We are, however, confronted with the same dilemma that has long faced linguists. The native speaker of any language forms his speech without any necessary awareness of the rules being used. Likewise, the rules of non-linguistic behavior are veiled by their very nature: they are *unconscious processes*. In both cases we must study these rules by analyzing their end products: language and behavior. As Watzlawick, Beavin, and Jackson state in

Pragmatics of Human Communication, the goal comes down to observing these processes exhibited through language and behavior in an attempt to identify a "complex pattern of redundancies" (p. 37). A good enough model, says Watzlawick, will give us the ability to evaluate, predict, and influence behavior.

In *The Structure of Magic, Vol. I*, Richard Bandler and John Grinder introduce a set of elegant tools for organizing and describing our observations. There are three mechanisms common to all model-building activities: *generalization*, *deletion*, and *distortion*. Bandler and Grinder call these the "universal human modeling processes."[3] These three processes operate at every stage in the construction and use of our models of the world. They underlie our abilities to concentrate, to plan and learn, and to dream. They become evident to the trained observer through a person's speech and behavior, and learning to detect and utilize these universal processes is a central theme of this book.

Generalization

The process of generalization provides part of the explanation of how we are able to learn as rapidly as we do. Many "new" behaviors, for example, are actually composed of bits and pieces of previously experienced behaviors that are similar to the new behavior. Because of this similarity, we are able to generalize from the experience of the old behavior, alleviating the need to learn the new behavior "from scratch." The ability to generalize from past experiences means that it is not necessary to expend great amounts of time and energy learning new behaviors. This same process is utilized in the learning of new concepts and in other activities associated with what we call "thinking." In essence, generalization eliminates the necessity to relearn a concept or behavior every time we are confronted with a variation of the original.

Generalization

One form of this process often taken for granted is our ability to learn a word-symbol, like the word "chair," and then apply the symbol to other forms with similar function. This ability to generalize promotes the rapid assimilation of diverse kinds of information.

Deletion

It has been reported that the human central nervous system is being fed more than two million pieces of information *every second*. Just in terms of efficiency, if every bit of this information had to be processed and used, the time and energy necessary would be astronomical! This is where the process of deletion comes in. Our central nervous system actually operates as a "screening mechanism" enabling us to function at peak efficiency. As Aldous Huxley says in *The Doors of Perception*, experience "has to be funneled through the reducing valve of the brain and nervous system. What comes out the other end is a measly trickle of the kind of consciousness that will help us to stay alive on the surface of this particular planet" (p. 23).

Obviously, our ability to delete portions of the barrage of input is essential to our survival.

Deletion

Paris in the
the spring.

A snake in the
the grass.

A kick in the
the rear.

One of my favorite examples of deletion is portrayed in the above three sentences. In order to make sense of what you see, there is a tendency to delete the portion of the sentence that doesn't make sense. Notice the extra "the" in each of the sentences. Many people have difficulty seeing it, even when it is pointed out to them. As we shall see, this process has some profound implications in the area of human communication.

Distortion

The third universal human modeling process forms the basis for most acts of creativity. Distortion is the process by which we alter our perceptions, changing our experience of sensory input. Using this process we both create and enjoy works of art, music, and literature. It also makes possible our ability to dream, fantasize, and plan for the future. By allowing us to manipulate our perceptions of reality, of the world as we *sense* it or *remember* it to be, distortion enables us to create totally unique variables. Some of our "creations" may even be outside the realm of possibility as defined by our model of reality. But whether it results in a "quantum leap" in our thinking or simply enables us to "interpret" a Picasso, distortion is an important process in our modeling of the world.

Distortion

The figure above represents a "visual paradox." Because it presents con-
flicting information, the observer finds himself attempting to make sense
of an apparent irrational figure. This *distortion* occurs because of the
capacity of the brain to take in certain kinds of information, in this case a
two-dimensional set of lines, and transform it into something that is nonexistent: a three-dimensional form.

These remarkable model-building processes of generalization, deletion,
and distortion, however, are double-edged. As important as they are to our
ability to learn, think, and create, these same processes can also cause pain
and suffering in an individual. How do these indispensable tools cause
pain? How do they limit perception and disallow behavior? How do they
become counter-productive to a person's normal living and growing? They
do these things by performing their functions just as they are designed.

The following examples will demonstrate how these processes can work both for and against the best interests of an individual.

Case Study

Several years ago, we had a client who demonstrated perfectly the duality in function of the universal human modeling processes. What follows are excerpts from some of our sessions that exemplify these processes in action.

As a child, Sharon had several very pleasant experiences in a particular reading group. These experiences were soon generalized to *all* reading and Sharon became an enthusiastic "bookworm." This can be considered a positive example of the process of generalization.

One of the reasons Sharon decided to come in for counseling was what she termed "a fear of men." This "fear" kept her from relaxing enough to have any close, affectionate relationships. In her words, "Men frighten me. I'm afraid all they want is to take advantage of me." We quickly uncovered where her fear had come from: Sharon recounted a severely traumatic experience she'd had with a man when she was a young teenager. From this one terrible experience she had begun to generalize about the "motives" of men. These generalizations had become a part of her model of the world and effectively prevented her from enjoying the close, loving relationship that she so dearly wanted. As with her experiences with reading, this modeling process occurred "automatically," completely out of her conscious awareness.

Assumptions are Generalizations

Some folks we know did an experiment with their bathroom door. Taking the doorknob from a regular door, they mounted it on a non-latching, one-way swinging door. To open their bathroom door, all you had to do was push on it; it would then swing closed automatically. The trick was that they placed the "fake" doorknob on the same side of the door as the hinges. The results of the experiment proved interesting.

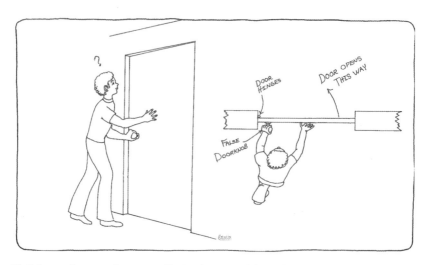

Children, they said, generally had no problem discovering the "trick" and were able to get into the bathroom. However, when adults tried the doorknob and found that the door wouldn't open, they *assumed* that it was either stuck or locked. Their assumption, of course, was based on generalizations from past experiences with locked and stuck doors. This part of their models of the world did not allow for the exploration necessary to discover the trick, and they consistently failed to gain entry without the "help" of their hosts.

One of the ways that Sharon was able to be such a good reader was her ability to keep noises and external visual stimuli from distracting her. She had learned to systematically delete from her awareness anything that would detract from her ability to concentrate on the book she was reading. This can be a very productive utilization of the process of deletion.

Selective attention is deletion

In the years following her traumatic encounter, Sharon also systematically deleted from her awareness the positive, normal responses of men who became genuinely interested in her. Her "selective attention" only allowed her to be aware of the things they did to "take advantage" of her. Because her model of the world did not include the possibility of warm, kind, and honest attention between men and women, she was not aware of these qualities when they were present in a male admirer. Without this awareness, no healthy relationship could develop.

Again, operating without conscious awareness, deletion can assist us by focusing our attention when necessary, as in the example of Sharon's reading. However, the same process can often be the major source of a person's emotional distress. It can create limitations on our models of the world that prevent us from being able to perceive what we need in order to achieve our goals.

Sharon loved to read novels. By creatively employing the process of distortion, she could transform words into full, rich experiences. She actually "lived" characters as she read about them. She felt their joys and sorrows, labored in the muddy fields, and had tea with the Queen. As a youngster, Sharon had learned to read words and then to distort them into images, feelings, sounds, tastes, and smells so vividly that they became "real" to her. She could talk about different times and faraway places as if she had actually been there. And she could equally well "project" herself into a history book or encyclopedia. This talent played an important part in her choice of career as a writer and lecturer.

Sharon also used the process of distortion as a means for explaining her "predicament" with men. Though her fear was a major factor, she attributed much of the problem to a series of "bad relationships." As she said, "If only those relationships had been different, if only they had given me what I wanted and needed, then I probably would be a lot happier now." Using the same process that she used to *place herself into* the characters she read about, Sharon indicated by those words that she had effectively *removed herself from* the external world during specific periods in her life.

In her model of the world, it was "relationships" that caused her problems. However, this indicates a distortion of her perception of the situation. A relationship is a *process* involving active participation.[4] By saying that "the relationships" hadn't given her what she wanted, she was ignoring her own responsibility and participation in the process of relating. She had *removed* herself from the role of participant and had become a helpless observer. This distortion, built into her model of the world, effectively prevented her from being able to change in ways that would make her more comfortable and happy. Not until she could *step back* into the process of relating would she be able to make those changes and regain a sense of control over her own life.

Fantasy is distortion

The construction of our models of the world may be what James Coleman (1972) is referring to when he says that an individual builds a "frame of reference" or "a set of assumptions concerning fact, possibility, and value." He describes how this "inner cognitive map" determines how a person will perceive reality and how he will behave. Of importance here is what happens when a person's map or model has built-in errors. As he says, "faulty assumptions have important implications for adjustive behavior." A person who follows this erroneous map "may bristle at nonexistent bogeymen and be unaware of real hazards. To the extent that his view is distorted, he will adjust to a world that does not exist, and will inevitably make miscalculations that will lead to failure and self devaluation" (p. 167).

Trust: Gaining Rapport

Who can deny that the important vector in any type of psychotherapeutic relationship is the establishment of good rapport?

William Kroger and William Fezler, *Hypnosis and Behavior Modification*

In his book *Persuasion and Healing*, Jerome Frank isolates some of the variables that make up a successful therapeutic relationship, especially aspects of the relationship that result in the patient's "susceptibility to the therapist's influence" (p. 197). Of particular interest here is the emphasis put on several variables: the client's expectations and his trust in the therapist, and what he calls "personal attributes of the therapist." Frank found that these factors greatly influence the outcome of therapy.

A study conducted by Strupp, Fox, and Lessler (1969) identified the patient's trust in the therapist as a singularly important variable. As they stated: "This faith in the integrity of the therapist as a person may be called the capstone of a successful therapeutic relationship subsuming other characteristics" (p. 36).

In any close or intimate relationship, trust becomes a primary element. This section will begin to explore the various ways this trust develops and the effects it has on the rapport so essential to an effective relationship.

As previously mentioned, Frank (1973) noted that particular attributes of the therapist himself are important ingredients of the therapeutic relationship. From questionnaires filled out by their patients, Frank found these attributes to include the therapist's ability to be a "keenly interested ... concerned listener ... who speaks one's language [and] makes sense" (p. 185). The development of trust, then, may begin when a person gets the sense that he is being understood, that he and the other person are "speaking the same language." Think for a moment about the people in your life whom you consider to be *influential*. This ability to influence you and others is based in large part on the trust given them by those who believe they are "understanding." Of course, this is an oversimplification. However, especially in the therapeutic setting, this trust is often a necessary condition for a successful therapeutic relationship. Trust must also exist between friends or the relationship falters. A business deal cannot be consummated unless there is a mutual trust based on the belief that each party is being understood by the other.

What is it about particularly influential individuals that leads to this trust? What observable behaviors do these wizards of communication exhibit that we might identify and use ourselves in our own professional and personal relationships? As these questions are answered, you will begin to discover some of the practical strategies for creating positive change.

Being Understood

One of the most important ingredients in being influential is the ability to elicit the belief that you understand. Understanding implies that you can "join" a person at his own model of the world. This is important because people tend to operate as if their model of the world *is* the *real* world. Understanding is the crucial bridge between our model of the world and theirs.

Logical Typing Errors

Gregory Bateson illustrates the distinction between "reality" and our models of reality with a menu card analogy.[5] We tend to operate on the assumption that a "thing" and its "name" are one and the same. Bateson calls this a "logical typing error." It is like walking into a restaurant, says Bateson, and being handed a menu card. Since the menu merely represents the food, we might consider it to be a map or model of reality. However, if we treat the menu like we often treat our own models of the world – as if it actually is reality – we would begin to eat the menu! As Bateson points out, "Expectably, communicating organisms ... will mistake map for territory" (1972, p. 402).

To take the metaphor a step further, sometimes we are surprised by the food we have ordered from the menu. When it arrives, we may not even like it, though we liked what was represented by the menu. Ideally, we would be able to go into a restaurant, stop by the kitchen, and sample the food before we decided. Even then, however, we couldn't be absolutely sure of what we would get when the waiter brought our food. But at least we might have a better idea.

We cannot actually "sample" reality as the metaphor suggests. All we ever have are menus: models of reality that we tend to believe *are* what they merely *represent*.

There are several ways you can "join" a person at his own model of the world. These will be covered in following sections and chapters. As you acknowledge an individual's model of the world by joining him with your language and with other behaviors that let him know that you understand, you pave the way for highly effective and influential communication to occur. This does not mean that you accept his model as your own, but rather that you instill the trust and rapport so important in close or intimate relationships and create the ideal climate for positive growth and change.

Constraints on the Model

> For every organism there are limitations and regularities which define what will be learned and under what circumstances this learning will occur.

> Gregory Bateson, *Steps to an Ecology of Mind*

The construction of our models of the world is not a haphazard, disorganized process. It is a highly efficient ongoing procedure that operates throughout our whole lifetime. The "information" used in the construction of our models, the experiences and memories of experiences that form the building blocks of the structure, are forced through certain constraints or "filters" on the model-building process. There are three constraints or filters that have been identified by Bandler and Grinder.[6] These are *neurological*, *social*, and *individual* constraints. Knowing the ways that these filters affect our models of the world can assist us in better observing the behavioral patterns that will enable us to both predict and influence with remarkable success the behavior of our clients, students, and others with whom we communicate.

Neurological Constraints

It is through our neurological makeup, our sense organs, and nerves that we initially receive information about the world. However, due to individual differences and the fact that "raw" information is translated into bioelectric impulses, we are inexorably separated from the "real world." Our neurology filters the experience and, because everyone's "filters" are slightly different, we can assume that everyone's model of the world will be different. This phenomenon underlies the idea that we do not react to the "real world" but rather to our own personal model of the world.

The Study of Perception

A term common to the study of perception is *absolute threshold*. This is the minimum amount of physical energy necessary to stimulate a sense organ into firing off a signal to the central nervous system (CNS). This means that there are potential sensory signals from our environment that are never even "received" or sensed. Our sensory organs not only channel information into our CNS but also effectively filter it as it comes in. For example, we know that there are sounds both above and below the ability of the human ear to hear, and we know that there are non-visible areas of the electromagnetic spectrum. This knowledge has been gained through the use of artificial mechanisms that translate or re-present these areas into perceivable stimuli. A good portion of our work as teachers and counselors is to operate much like those machines. That is, we work to represent aspects of the environment that they are filtering out or deleting from their experience. There will be more on that in upcoming sections.

Difference threshold is another term used in the study of perception. This is the minimum amount of stimulation necessary to be able to detect a difference between two similar stimuli. This just noticeable difference (JND) supports the notion that our receptor organs act as filters to our perception of the world.

Another important concept in the study of perception is the fact that our sensory mechanisms operate on a process called *recurrent inhibition*. Because of this neural mechanism, we tend to receive information from our senses primarily about *changes* in our environment rather than about constant or unchanging aspects of experience. One of the reasons for including a good bottle of wine with a meal is to stimulate our gustatory–olfactory sensing organs between bites of food. The wine literally changes the environment in our mouths so that each bite will taste just as savory as the first.

Recurrent inhibition is what underlies the tendency to cease paying attention to static, unchanging aspects of our environment. It is interesting to speculate about how this neurological mechanism might affect our experience of the world on a broader scale. Noam Chomsky (see Chapter 3), quoting Viktor Shklovskij, writes:

People living at the seashore grow so accustomed to the murmur of the waves that they never hear it. By the same token, we scarcely ever hear the words which we utter ... We look at each other, but we do not see each other anymore. Our perception of the world has withered away; what has remained is mere recognition. (1972, pp. 24–25)

Our sensory systems can provide us with very pleasant experiences in many ways. Movies, which are actually only rapidly flashed "still" pictures, give us the illusion of motion. We can also experience strong emotional feelings while sitting in a theater watching and listening to a film. It is important to understand that these same abilities, these neurological processes that enable us to have pleasant experiences, also operate at times to give us pain by *limiting* our perceptions and our ability to adequately respond to our environment.

As the discussion of these processes continues, we hope to demonstrate that there are consistencies in how people experience the world and how they create their models of what they experience. These consistencies can assist us in more effectively communicating with them. By enabling us to predict and influence behavior, observing and utilizing these consistencies can help us assist the people we live and work with in making different choices about how to feel and how to respond, choices that will enhance a positive and enriched perception of the world.

The diagram below shows the first step in the formulation of our models of the world. Raw experience is filtered through our sensory organs (neurological constraints). The experience is "transformed" into a neurological model including four basic parameters: vision, feeling, sound, and smell and taste. Following the model proposed by Bandler and Grinder, these are labeled, respectively, V for vision, K for feelings, A for sounds, and OG for smell and taste.[7] For every moment there is one complete "set" of these experiences. Each of these sets is called a *4-tuple*. For purposes of the diagram below, we will show taste and smell using "OG" to stand for olfactory and gustatory processes. In Chapter 2 we will adopt the alternate notation using just "O" to simplify the model.

Creating the 4-tuple

Social Constraints

Another way we create differences in our models is through social constraints, what Bandler and Grinder (1975) call social genetic factors "to remind the reader that social constraints ... have as profound effect on shaping their perceptions as do neurological constraints" (p. 19). This filter might be thought of as the second level in the model-building process, coming just after neurological constraints. The primary example of social constraints is *language*, which operates on our models of the world in two primary and apparently opposite ways. One way is to *enhance* and the other is to *limit* our perception of the world around us. It does this by encoding perceptual phenomena into labels (words) that are manipulated by the mind in its efforts to make sense out of experience.[8] For example, Eskimos have some seventy different words for *snow*. (This is actually a myth! Please see footnote.)[9] They are able to make distinctions about the quality and structure of snow that are beyond the abilities of most individuals in the rest of the world. Obviously this has great survival value to the Eskimo culture. This deeply rooted social constraint, exhibited in the Eskimo language, expands their models of the world to include perceptions that people from other linguistic backgrounds are unable to observe.

An interesting phenomenon occurs when someone becomes fluent in a language different from his native tongue. As J. Samuel Bois, the general semanticist, observes in *The Art of Awareness*, "I don't see the same things, don't observe the same events, when I change from my French to my English brain." He goes on to say, "Changing my language changes me as an observer. It changes my world at the same time" (p. 20).

The diagram below shows the language component being added to the 4-tuple. This either accentuates certain aspects of the neurological model or deletes or distorts it. It can enhance perception as in the case of the Eskimos (continuing the "myth" from above). Even though we could stand side-by-side with an Eskimo and look at the snow, we would not "see" the same thing because our models of the world are different. The same is true of individuals who come into therapy. As we shall see, it is often through their language that their limited or distorted perception of the world can be known. With this knowledge we can assist them in learning new ways to *talk about* their experiences, ways that will ultimately change their models of the world.

Adding language

There are other forms of social constraint that affect a person's modeling process. As Coleman (1972) puts it, "his personality development reflects both the larger society in which he lives – its institutions, traditions, values, ideas, and technologies – and the immediate family and other interpersonal relationships" (p. 78). Social customs and conventions are learned and integrated by an individual in much the same ways language is learned. By watching and listening to others and by being corrected when we "error," we come to know what is expected by social convention. Like language, these social rules vary from generation to generation and between the subcultures that make up the larger society. Much like rules that govern language, these social constraints are powerful filters on our models of the world, affecting both perception and behavior. As the illustrations below will demonstrate, social constraints form some of the boundaries between what we believe to be possible and impossible, good and bad, appropriate and inappropriate, and so on.

In the recent past, both in the United States and in parts of Western Europe, it was customary for a woman to faint or "swoon" in certain situations. In movies from that period, there was always someone in the crowd ready with smelling salts to help revive the distressed maiden. The situations in which swooning occurred were highly standardized, and the behavior was limited to only a few subcultures here and in Europe.

Another highly regulated phenomenon rarely witnessed today was the "duel." This formal fight between two individuals followed a specific form dictated by social custom. Both parties played out each step of the prescribed sequence of responses. The form was rigid and predictable, and everyone knew what was expected.

Social constraints

A more current example of social constraints concerns socially imposed "rules" governing direct eye contact.[10] There are subcultures in the United States which believe that if one man stares directly into the eyes of another man, it is a "challenge," much like the traditional "glove-in-the-face slap" that initiated the duel ritual. In these situations, again highly regulated by custom, there are specific things that each man is expected to do. The challenge is either accepted or declined, depending on the response of the second man to the initiating stare.

Problems may result if two or more individuals are combined from different subcultures with different rules or customs. In an institutional setting, for example, where many differing subcultures are forced to co-mingle, inability to predict expected responses creates the potential for very volatile interactions. For those responsible for maintaining order, the process of "keeping the peace" can become a laborious and sometimes harrowing experience.

Any time we are confronted with a situation where two models differ, as in the above example, it becomes crucial to determine what the *rules* are for each of the models. These social constraints on the models, properly utilized, are invaluable in the process of gaining rapport, in "speaking the same language" as the parties involved. Using these rules can help create the trust and free-flowing communication necessary for successful positive interventions. Understanding the impact of social constraints on the communication process is one of the ways of orienting yourself to the inevitable differences in each individual's model of the world. Identifying and then honoring these constraints will prevent them from blocking the communication process.

Individual Constraints

As pointed out by Lucy Ferguson in *Personality Development*, "personality is a term that has been defined more variously than perhaps any other general concept in psychology" (p. 2). Taking into account an individual's genetic makeup, Ferguson makes a valid argument for an interpretation of personality based on knowledge of that individual's *personal history*. Individual constraints, the third in the series discussed here, are the direct result of personal experiences. Taken as a whole, they are what form a person's "historical background."

Individual constraints are based on both neurological and social constraints, the two underlying filters of experience. As a person continues the process of construction and modification of his model of the world, it is individual constraints that form the fabric of his belief and value systems. They play an important part in what makes up the "rose" in a person's "rose-colored glasses." It is personal history in part that explains why a ghetto youth is less likely to score as high on the Stanford–Binet intelligence test as a youngster from an "upper class" family. These constraints also account for part of the diversity of scores on tests like the Minnesota Multiphasic Personality Inventory (MMPI).

Important to our understanding of individual models of the world is the concept of *internally generated stimuli*. As previously mentioned, for every moment in time, we create a 4-tuple of experience. This includes the parameters of visual experience (V); feelings, which include tactile, proprioceptive, and somatic experiences (K); the experience of sound (A); and smell and taste, also known as olfactory and gustatory experience (OG). We also have an immense collection of stored experiences called memories. These memories can be manipulated, shuffled, and reorganized in very creative ways, something we generally call "thinking." Thinking, however, is merely *synthetic experience*, extrapolations and recombinations of current and previously experienced material in new and unique ways.

It is possible to substitute synthesized elements for other sensory-based experiences in a 4-tuple. In other words, at any given moment, a person may experience combinations of internally generated pictures, images, feelings, sounds, smells, and tastes along with stimuli of external origin. The smell of a Christmas tree, for example, may originate in the external environment. However, it may instantaneously elicit internally generated visual memories, feelings, and sounds associated with that particular smell. These synthesized elements in the 4-tuple are based on a person's previous experiences of his past personal history, in combination with various wants and needs of the moment. Synthetic experiences are also subject to the universal modeling processes of generalization, deletion, and distortion.

Internal experience

"Emotionally-laden" experiences are often elicited by cues in the external environment. They may be pleasant, as in the above example, or they may be devastating. An example of an internally generated dysfunctional response to external cues is described in a transcript of a counseling session in Chapter 4 (beginning on page 153).

The diagram below shows the 4-tuple going through the Individual filter. It is at this point in the formation of the experience, the perception of "one moment in time," that a person adds synthesized elements to the 4-tuple. The model shows these internally generated experiences pairing up with their external counterpart on the 4-tuple. For each element in a 4-tuple, a person is generally only *aware* of one aspect, either the internal or the external experience, but not both at the same time. It is also important to note that although there will always be input from the external environment (except in cases of neurological damage, such as blindness), there does not necessarily have to be an associated internally generated experience for each element in the 4-tuple. For simplicity, the model below shows a complete set of these "synthesized" experiences hitching a ride under the external 4-tuple.

As we shall see in later chapters, people can systematically delete one particular element from their 4-tuples. The ability of a therapist to detect and utilize this kind of information when working with an individual can greatly expedite the process of therapeutic growth and change. The example on page 153 demonstrates how this information can be effectively used.

As the diagram below shows, the 4-tuples are finally collected in the Memory Box. The repository for all experiences, it represents our personal history, our composite model of the world. This collection of experiences does much to shape our thinking and our perception of the world around us. Information for synthetic experiences in this simple diagram comes from the Memory Box through the Memory Tube. Again, this information can be in the form of a complete internally generated 4-tuple, or it can be single elements from the various stored 4-tuples that "replace" one or more of the pieces of external origins. When an individual is accessing a memory – such as what color his kitchen is – the formal notation attaches a superscript r (V^r) to denote those portions of the 4-tuple that are *remembered* experience. In addition, we also have the capacity to generate novel new internal experiences, such as imagining what the kitchen would look like painted blue. In these cases we use the superscript c (V^c) to denote an internally *constructed* component of the 4-tuple. These distinctions along with the *internal–external* notations described at the beginning of this chapter become extremely important when we begin to utilize models of a person's experience to assist them to change mental *strategies* (specific sequences of mental steps involved in solving problems, making decisions, creating, learning, etc.) that limit their ability to feel or act the way they want.[11]

A complete diagram showing three processes is presented in Appendix A.

Adding individual constraints

Meta-States

Susie Linder-Pelz (2011) writes about how the meta-states model developed by Hall (2002 [1995]) describes how people process information. She explains that people "layer" information from the outside world and then "frame or *meta-state* that information as they feed back to themselves more information about that information; that is, they feed back to themselves layer upon layer of ideas, beliefs and understandings. Each new progressive layer sets the frame for the previous layers. Then people *feed forward* that information back down the 'levels' of their mind, brain and neurology. This literally *in-forms*: it forms the individual on the inside and manifests as emotions or somatic movements in the body and in behaviour" (p. 81, original emphasis).

This is important because it underscores the fact that *perception* is not a one-way process. Indeed, our "perceptions" aggregate and interact in such a way as to influence both future experience and past memories.

When we communicate with people, when we are successful in creating therapeutic changes, or when we are teaching something new, we always begin at the neurological level with the sound of our voices and the look and feel of our actions. When intervention occurs at the linguistic level (see Chapter 3), we are operating on a person's 4-tuple at the level of social constraints. At the level of individual constraints, we assist people in understanding how their models of the world are dysfunctional, how they are causing unnecessary pain and hardship in their lives, or how they block the awareness of alternative thoughts, feelings, or actions.

Ultimately, any learning or therapeutic experience that is successful becomes a part of a person's personal history. Filed into his "Memory Box," the new model will begin to shape thinking and perception in new, positive, and healthy ways.

It is important to point out, as did Bandler and Grinder,[12] that this discussion of constraints on the model-building processes is not meant to be a comprehensive presentation, nor is it meant to imply that there are distinct divisions between the three constraints. They actually overlap. The purpose of this book is to present the reader with *models* for perceiving, predicting, and influencing behavior. They are useful for these purposes even though they are inaccurate: a model merely *represents* what it is modeling.

Complex Equivalence

One example of overlapping constraints involves language. Due to the influence of neurological and individual constraints, internal representations of language (social constraints) are different for everybody. For every word learned, everyone has a somewhat different internal experience. These specific experiences associated with words are called *complex equivalence*.[13] Usually the subtleties between people's understanding of words are irrelevant. However, there are words that sometimes lead to misunderstanding between people. Words like *love, relationship, partnership, fear, power, trust, respect*, and any expressions linked with a person's perception of himself and his environment are critical to the process of communication, as the example below demonstrates.

Complex equivalence

It is important when you are learning the basic principles of effective communication to drop the assumption that you already know what words such as those listed above mean. Your "knowing" is based on your own model of the world which is also subject to the processes of generalization, deletion, and distortion, as well as to neurological, social, and individual constraints. Rather than presuming that your understanding of these words is the same as the speaker's, it is often advisable to ask for his own definitions. This may keep you from becoming trapped by your own model of the world. By more fully understanding what the speaker is saying, you are more likely to gain rapport and be more influential in your communication with him. Specific techniques for asking for a person's definitions of these words, as well as some linguistic clues for when more information is needed, are given in Chapter 3.

Summary

I do not attempt to define what a human being *is*, I describe what a human being *does*.

Joseph S. Bois, *The Art of Awareness*

[W]e are looking for pragmatic redundancies; we know that they will not be simple, static magnitudes or qualities, but patterns analogous to the mathematical concept of function.

Paul Watzlawick, Janet Beavin, and Don Jackson, *Pragmatics of Human Communication*

In dealing with communication, it is important to note the distinction made by Walzlawick et al. (1967) that *all* behavior is communication. There are actually two kinds of communicative behavior. One encompasses observable patterns of interaction, primarily speech and overt gestures. The other is less obvious communication that goes on *inside* each of us all the time. All communication, whether overtly exhibited or internally experienced, affects us in observable ways. It is the observation and utilization of specific communicative behaviors that make up the major theme of this book.

Once we begin to explore the ways we make sense of the myriad experiences we call "living," many behavioral patterns become evident. Grinder and Bandler's "human modeling processes" afford us an organizational basis from which to explore differences between what people experience (the territory) and how they make sense of those experiences (their map or model of the world).

Supported by evidence from neurological studies, we extend this model-building behavior to include three constraints: neurological, social, and individual. By understanding that these mechanisms are important in the creation of an individual's model and in that person's representation of "who" he is, we begin the first step in gaining the rapport and trust so important to influential and therapeutic communications. Recognizing that each person creates a different model of the world enables us to cherish rather than judge or fear those differences. It is those differences that make each of us unique and create the amazing and wonderful diversity of personality we encounter within and between societies.

We share a universal linguistic convention: understanding presupposes consistencies in language at many levels. It is through these consistent patterns of behavior that we are able to survive in and perpetuate a society. These same behaviors provide clues as to how an individual creates not only joy and understanding but also pain and confusion in his daily life.

Some elements of communication are within our conscious control, but most are completely outside our conscious awareness. As we begin to attend to communication as a presentation of unique personal models, many of the idiosyncrasies that produce miscommunication and misunderstanding become, instead, tools for even deeper and more profound communication. The more astute we become at seeing, hearing, and feeling the total messages being sent, the better able we will be to perceive what is really meant. This awareness will also enable us to better use our own channels of communication to express what we need and want, not only to others but also *within* ourselves.

This book is a presentation of various models of human behavior. These models can be extremely useful as tools when used to understand, predict, and shape the human interactions we call communication. But these models can also be very limiting if we forget that they are not actually reality. We must keep in mind the idea stated so well by Edward Hall:

> All theoretical models are incomplete. By definition, they are abstractions and therefore leave things out. What they leave out is as important as, if not more important than, what they do not, because it is what is left out that gives structure and form to the system. (1976, p. 14)

Notes to Chapter 1

1. It is important here to bring up a discussion by Tosey and Mathison (2009) regarding representationalism. Quoting Brockman (1977), they write: "I discovered that when I see something, or hear a sound, or taste, it is my brain, or perhaps I should better say 'mind' – it is I who create an image in the modality of the appropriate sense organ. My image is my aggregation and organization of information about the perceived object, aggregated and integrated by me according to rules of which I am totally unconscious" (p. 66). When we created the 4-tuple diagrams later in this chapter and at Appendix A, we are providing the reader with a "visual metaphor" of the process by which we transform sensory input and codify it into a "map" of "reality." However, as Tosey and Mathison (2009) point out, "our perceptions do not merely receive and represent an 'external' world; instead they create our experience" (pp. 66–67). Our use of the term representation and especially representational system later in

this work includes this complex interaction of mind-map-territory which does not reflect the representationalist view that what we call experience is simply a re-presentation of the world in the sense of its being a replica.

2.   For the purpose of this work, the distinction between "ourselves" and our surrounding environment is a functional one. It does not imply that other ways of describing the relationship do not exist. As Jung points out in Psychological Types (1971 [1923]), psychology focuses on internal processes that operate inside both the subject and the observer. Therefore, "the observer should be ... able to see not only subjectively but also objectively. The demand that he should see only objectively is quite out of the question, for it is impossible. We must be satisfied if he does not see too subjectively" (p. 9). Roger Walsh (1979) also makes a contribution to the discussion: "What can be known is the interaction between the observer and the observed and never the independent properties of the observed alone. All observation is a function of the observer, and thus the known universe is inextricably linked with consciousness" (p. 180).

3.   Bandler and Grinder (1975) discus many of the models presented in this work. The "universal human modeling processes" are presented on pp. 14–18. We highly recommend any of Bandler and Grinder's books (see Bibliography).

4.   This is a linguistic form called a "nominalization." See Chapter 3 for a complete discussion of this and other linguistic indications of the structure of a person's model of the world.

5.   See Bateson's discussion in Steps to an Ecology of Mind (1972) on the "theory of logical types," beginning on p. 280.

6.   Bandler and Grinder's rendition appears in The Structure of Magic, Vol. I (1975, pp. 8–13). Watzlawick et al. (1967) give the definition of constraint as follows: "According to information theory, stochastic processes show redundancy or constraint, two terms which can be used interchangeably with the concept of pattern" (p. 34, original emphasis). As used in this book, then, constraints are patterns that operate on the model-building processes. They can be conceptualized as a "grid" or "filter" through which information is processed on the way to becoming an experience.

7. See Bandler and Grinder (1976, pp. 4–12).

8. Whorf's "linguistic-relativity hypotheses" is a well-formed presentation of the idea that thought is relative to the language in which it is constructed. In *Language, Thought, and Reality* (1956), he proposes that it is the structure of language that causes culturally seated differences in perception.

9. See Bandler and Grinder (1979, p. 15). We offer our sincere apologies for our uncritical acceptance and resulting perpetration of the anthropological hoax of the Eskimo words for snow. The citation has been intentionally left in this revised edition specifically to make this point. We invite the reader to type those italicized words into any search engine and read some of the informative and often humorous articles about this urban myth. You can also find an entertaining examination of the topic in Geoffrey Pullman's *The Great Eskimo Vocabulary Hoax* (1976). Pullman accuses us of "intellectual sloth" (p. 171) and writes: "Sadly, the academic profession shows a strong tendency to create stable and self-sustaining but completely false legends of its own, and hang on to them grimly, transmitting them from article to article and from textbook to textbook like software viruses spreading between students' Macintoshes" (p. 159).

10. This is somewhat different from the eye contact rule discussed in association with the visual communication category in Chapter 2. However, it is not unusual for conflict to occur as a result of an encounter between someone operating with the social eye contact model and someone else operating out of the visual system.

11. Dilts and DeLozier (2000) link the process of identifying strategies in early NLP's development with its eventual name. They write: "By observing patterns of people's language and eye movements, Bandler, Grinder and their students began to recognize specific and consistent sequences in the way that people used their sensory modalities in order to remember, make decisions, learn, or accomplish other cognitive tasks. It was the attempt to analyze and map these sequences of sensory activity that spurred the name 'Neuro-Linguistic Programming'" (p. 1318).

12. See Bandler and Grinder (1975, p. 19, fn. 2).

13. From Bandler et al. (1976) comes the following definition: "*Complex Equivalence* is the relationship between a word or set of words and some experience which those words name" (p. 90, original emphasis).

Chapter 2
The Communication Categories Model

Sorcerers say that we are inside a bubble. It is a bubble into which we are placed at the moment of our birth. At first the bubble is open, but then it begins to close until it has sealed us in. That bubble is our perception. We live inside that bubble all of our lives. And what we witness on its round walls is our own reflection.

Carlos Castaneda, *Tales of Power*

We have found that by closely observing people, behavioral patterns become apparent. These patterns are communicated to us both verbally and non-verbally and may be expressed as a tendency to use certain forms of language or to maintain habitual ways of moving, standing, or sitting. There are additional characteristics that come across as we observe individuals in social situations where they may adopt a habitual set of behaviors when communicating with others. In this chapter, we will explore some of these patterns of behavior and group them into four distinct *communication categories*.

Representational Systems

Perception is an exciting area of study in the field of psychology. As discussed in the previous chapter, because neurological input forms the basic building blocks of our models of the world, there are many different ways to describe the process we call perception. What follows is based on the neurological model presented in Chapter 1.

There are five primary ways humans experience the world. Barring neurological damage, we can see, feel, hear, smell, and taste. Each one of these sensory inputs has physical places in our brains to which the experience is sent, processed, and recorded. This *assimilation* of the initial input transforms the experience into something different from the original stimulus. What we actually perceive are representations or *models* of what each of our sensory organs transmits to us. These individual models of assimilation are called *representational systems*.[1]

At any moment we are receiving and processing input from all of our senses, even when we are not consciously aware of it. Each "slice out of time" is composed of the elements that make up the 4-tuple (4T) described in Chapter 1. Every 4T includes each of the representational systems: sight is the visual system (V), feeling is the kinesthetic system (K), hearing is the auditory system (A), and smell and taste make up the "olfactory" system (O).[2] The 4T is written like this:

‹V K A O›

External V, internal K, A, O

Dilts and DeLozier (2000) point out that representational systems are not simply re-presentations of experience. They "include the entire system of processes relating to a particular sensory modality including input, processing, storage, retrieval, and output" (p. 1098). In order to differentiate between experience of external origins and synthetic or internally generated experience, the superscripts ^{e} for *external* and ^{i} for *internal* can be used. For example, you may be reading a magazine and turn a page to see a full-color picture of a sailboat (V^e). This in turn may instantly elicit the memory of the feeling of a boat rocking under your feet (K^i), the sound of sails slapping in the wind (A^i), and the smell and taste of the ocean (O^i). The 4T for that complete experience would be written like this:

$$V^e \, K^i \, A^i \, O^i$$

This formal shorthand can help make the observation and discussion of communicative behaviors easier and more concise.

The Digital Representational System

During the process of building our models of the world, language and other social constraints are attached to our experiences. The collection of word symbols and the rules that govern their use make up a unique and distinct representational system. Unlike the systems in the 4T, the *digital system*, made up of language, is not an analog system: it is not directly related to any of our sensory organs. Language is the only system that can represent all of the other representational systems. It can create models of (re-present) each system including itself. There is evidence that this more recently evolved modeling tool may be subjugated to the analog systems, however. The following description from Watzlawick et al. demonstrates this relationship:

> Children, fools and animals have always been credited with particular intuition regarding the sincerity of human attitudes, for it is easy to profess something verbally, but difficult to carry a lie into the realm of the analogic. (1967, p. 63)

The goal of this book is to increase your ability to detect and utilize patterns of behavior that occur both within an individual and between people as they interact. Language, the digital representational system, is able to represent all of the systems used by people to create and communicate their experiences of the world. Because of this, it provides an especially effective tool for alerting an attentive listener to important information about a speaker's model of the world.

Differing patterns of word usage are demonstrated in the following five sentences. Take a moment to read each one carefully. Pay particular attention to how each one elicits a somewhat different subjective experience.

Sentence 1
I looked down from where I sat at the head of the long, dark, oak table, and it seemed to me that they should all know better than to think the thoughts I saw clearly reflected on their bright, smiling faces.

Sentence 2
I was suddenly aware of that helpless feeling again, that gnawing sensation in my belly, and, lowering my eyes, I knelt down gripping at the smooth, comforting folds of my robe.

Sentence 3
That rings a bell with me, too; it would be good if we could tune ourselves into your program without altering our tempo and thus create more harmonious relationships within the group.

Sentence 4
The salty sea breezes mixed with the sweet scent of delicate flowers, but the nearby marsh reeked of pungent, sulfurous earth that kept threatening to spoil an otherwise savory afternoon.

Sentence 5
It is quite possible that the current situation could be improved, if not by moderating, then perhaps by rearticulating the response argument in order to preclude less desirable results.

Each of the above sentences evokes one of the representational systems. Through the consistent use of certain words and phrases in each sentence, the reader is led into an experience – an "understanding" – that taps portions of his model of the world associated with his sensory systems. This is true except, of course, for the last sentence.

The first sentence, for example, illustrates the visual representational system. Many readers find that they can actually "see" the table, the faces, and the thoughts. By going through their own *personal history* – the collection of all past experiences stored in the mind – they create for themselves internal experiences similar to the one described. In the same way, most people are able to create "feelings" from the second sentence, which exemplifies the kinesthetic system. This creative construction of internal experiences in response to words plays a crucial role in the process of communication.

Emotions

The kinesthetic representational system includes several important distinctions. Sensory inputs from the body are classed as *somatic* sensations. These include the *exteroceptive* sensations of temperature, touch, and pain; *proprioceptive* sensations from deeper in our muscles, tendons, and joints that keep us informed as to body position, vibrations, and deep pain and pressure; and *visceral* sensations of pain and fullness from internal organs.

In our language, however, we have identified other kinds of "feelings," those we call *emotions*. When someone says, "I was hurt," he may be talking about pressure or pain on his skin, or he may be talking about some "internal state" called an emotion.

Actually, the two meanings are very similar. To be "hurt" emotionally is a composite of several somatic sensations. For example, there may be a tightening around the eyes and face, changes in posture, stresses on deep muscle tissue, tendons, and joints, and often accompanying input from the viscera in the form of tightening or contractions. This sensory input is combined with other thought processes and is then labeled as emotional "hurt." Because of this close link with somatic sensations, it is useful to consider that those feelings we call emotions are actually *derived feelings* or, in the formal notation, K^d.

The third sentence elicits experiences associated with the auditory system, and the fourth the olfactory–gustatory system. Though taste and smell are two distinct sensory mechanisms, they are grouped together for simplicity. Generally, unless you are a gourmet chef or wine connoisseur, your model of the world probably does not contain as many distinctions in the olfactory representational system as in the other systems. In fact, the visual and kinesthetic appear to be two of the most often used systems in Western cultures.

Olfactory–gustatory distinctions

The fifth sentence is unique because none of the words presuppose any of the sensory-based systems. This is an example of purely digital information. In such a case, it is entirely up to the reader to "understand," using whatever system is best for him. This process will be explored in great detail in this chapter.

Language is used to communicate various aspects of our experience of the world to each other. By creating internally generated experiences, or *referents*, in response to the words we read or hear, we are able to understand what is being said. However, this "synthetic" experience can also operate in ways that prevent us from experiencing fully what the speaker or writer intends to communicate. Since our process of understanding is internally generated, it is affected by the universal human modeling processes of generalization, deletion, and distortion. Because we each have unique models of the world, the following axiom must be considered important to the study of communication:

The *meaning* of any communication is defined by the *response* it elicits.

Predicate Preference

When listening to a person talk, sometimes a pattern becomes evident, a pattern of *predicate preference*. These descriptive words and phrases – primarily verbs, adverbs, and adjectives – often presuppose one of the representational systems. As you listen to a person talk over a period of time, you may discover that there are times when a majority of the predicates he uses refer to one system more often than any of the others. This person is choosing, usually at an unconscious level, to isolate one system from his ongoing "stream" of 4Ts. Then, using the digital system, he identifies that system by the words he selects to communicate with. This is important, because it indicates to you *how* that person is making sense of his experience. It is a clue to the person's model of the world, and it may also indicate what type of sensory experience he is most likely to notice.

We have identified four primary patterns of predicate preference. These are visual, kinesthetic, auditory, and digital (non-sensory). Because these patterns are often habitually utilized by the people with whom we interact, we will continue to concentrate on these four representational systems in this book.

Preferred Representational Systems

This more frequent use of one system over the others is called a person's *preferred representational system* (PR or PRS).[3] Its use can be thought of as habitual, and it often becomes particularly evident during situations that are stressful for the individual. This system is usually the one a person makes the most distinctions in. It is the system used most often by him to consciously and unconsciously represent and understand his experiences. One excellent example of how the preferred system operates is demonstrated by Roger Shepard, a Professor of Psychology at Stanford University. Following an extensive description of his primary visual "creative thinking processes," Shepard states:

> That in all of these sudden illuminations my ideas took shape in a primarily visual–spatial form without. So far as I can introspect, any verbal intervention is in accordance with what has always been my preferred mode of thinking. (1978, p. 183)

Another fine example of preferred representational systems took place while we were sitting with some friends one evening on a deck overlooking a beautiful stretch of the Pacific Ocean. Filled with the moment, we began to take turns describing our experiences. The following three quotations are more or less representative of what was actually said.

Susan

> I love the view. Look at the fantastic red and purple colors in the clouds where the sun just went down and how clearly they reflect in the water over there.

In the above example, Susan's predicates consistently reflect the visual representational system. Specifically, the visual predicates are: verbs – "look," "reflect"; adverbs – "clearly"; adjectives – "red," "purple." Also nouns like "view" and "colors" indicate the visual system. This person's description of the moment can create a "picture" in the listener's mind. It is an important indication of the part of the experience that is most important to Susan. People who consistently use this mode of expression will often use phrases like: "I see what you mean" and "Let me see if I can remember."

Thomas

> Right now I'm feeling very warm, almost radiant, towards all of you. I feel as though I've been in touch with each of you today in a special way, and sitting here with you all so close enhances that feeling.

This person places a great deal of emphasis on feelings, emotions, and other kinesthetic aspects of the experience. The kinesthetic predicates are: verbs – "feeling," "feel," "been in touch," "sitting"; adverbs – "warm," "radiant," "close." Common phrases used by people who speak from this system are: "Can you handle it?" and "I feel pretty comfortable with the situation now."

Mark

> I was noticing how, as the sun went down, everyone's voice got quieter, almost as if the change in the tone of the scenery was being echoed by our voices. I like days like this; it reminds me of a tune my father used to play on the guitar.

Auditory predicates characterize Mark's description. They include verbs like "echoed" and "play" (the guitar) and adverbs like "quieter." Other words auditory in nature are "voice" and "tone." Someone with a highly developed auditory representational system may make statements like: "That shirt is too loud for me" and "Does that sound good to you?"

Of course, a purely digital representation of the experience above might be, "I'm thinking that we're all of the same mind this evening, that we share a common bond, and that this makes this moment more meaningful." The digital predicates include: verbs – "thinking" and "share"; adverbs – "all of the same mind" and "common bond"; and the adjective – "meaningful". This person would be likely to use phrases such as, "I will ponder what you said," and, "I think I understand your meaning."

Leading by a Nose

In animals like dogs and cats, the olfactory system is crucial for their survival. In humans, however, it is less important. Though we probably make fewer distinctions in this system than in the others, it is very likely our most efficient *lead system*. A lead system is the representational system that is used to gain access to information stored in our minds. For example, we can search through our memories visually, like flipping through a series of slides; we can grope around, trying to get a feel for the answer to a hard question; or we can stammer as we desperately try to remember the name of an important person by going through a series of, "It sounds like ... and rhymes with ..."

Because olfactory input does not go through the same neurological processing on the way to the brain as the other systems, it tends to operate more efficiently as a lead system, often at an unconscious level.[4] Have you ever walked into a room and suddenly found yourself remembering some past event and then realized it was a smell in the room that almost instantaneously *led* you to the memory?

This system has also not escaped linguistic modeling. Several common phrases that utilize the olfactory system are: "It's bitter cold outside" and "That was tastefully done."

Use of representational systems is one of the ways people change their sensory input from the world into a model or a re-presentation of the world. Representational systems not only indicate the *process* by which individuals formally create their models but also provide us with a format by which we can understand how and what they experience. By listening carefully to the words people use, it is possible to identify patterns in their language that may indicate preference for one representational system over the others. Preferred representational systems are one of the most systematic ways in which people's models of the world differ. As we continue to demystify the processes of communication we will attend to these differences.

Utilizing the Language of the Representational Systems

In Chapter 1 it was suggested that everyone creates a model of the world and that due to differences in neurological, social, and individual constraints, everyone's model is different. Individual language patterns can assist us in determining what some of those differences are. Someone who occasionally says, "Yes, I see what you mean," is giving you a marvelous piece of information about how this person is making sense of what you are saying. Knowing this, you can frame your own language in such a way that you *match* that person's model. By using more visual predicates, you can help him to "see" even more "clearly" what you are talking about. By the same token, someone who says, "I don't quite grasp your meaning," may respond positively to a different linguistic pattern. Rather than trying to "paint a picture" for him with your words, it might be more effective to "grapple with the concepts" and "put them into pieces" that are "easier to get a handle on."

One way to think about preferred representational systems is to consider that each system has its own "language." This means that there are several different languages that are "foreign" to one another. By being able to understand and speak to a person using his own "language," you heighten the sense of rapport between you and pave the way for the trust that is so important to any close relationship.[5] Another way to think about predicate preference is to imagine how a blind person might perceive an elephant in comparison to a sighted person. You can be sure that their linguistic descriptions would demonstrate the differences.

Even though a person demonstrates a preference for one of the representational systems, it does not mean that he does not use the other systems too. On the contrary, we all use all of the systems all of the time. It has been our observation, however, that whether out of habit, in response to stressful situations, or in other areas of interaction, people tend to depend on their preferred system, the system in which they can make the most distinctions about the world. It also appears that, in some people, this system changes depending on the specific situation or context confronting them.

Stress

Fire engines clanged and wailed in the streets below, and people screamed unintelligible words from the buildings across the boulevard. The smell of smoke was getting more intense – that was probably what woke him up. Fire!

The image of burning buildings, flaming stairwells, and smoke-clogged hallways set him into a panic. He ran into the main hallway and started choking from the smoke he thought he could see there. He began looking frantically for a way out, trying to visualize where the fire escapes were.

Someone came up behind him and tapped him on the shoulder, saying, "Everyone's gone down the back way. Follow me!" Then he ran off, leading the way, assuming he was being followed. But the panic-struck man didn't turn and follow. He was still busy trying to remember, trying to visualize where he had seen an escape route. In his frenzy *he never even felt the touch nor did he hear the words* from behind him!

Often people under stress will turn to the representational system they trust the most. They may even delete other systems from their conscious awareness, thereby limiting their ability to respond. It is tragic because during just those times they need all the sensory input and all the awareness they can get! People coming into therapy who are under great stress in their lives are often extremely limited in their awareness of their problems and in their choices concerning how to behave. It is possible they are blocked by their inability to create new choices or to even perceive alternatives because the choices and perceptions lie outside the range of the system into which they have retreated.

The language of the representational systems can work for you in two ways. Besides indicating how a person is making sense of his experience, it can also provide an extremely effective method for gaining rapport with that person. This can be demonstrated by using the following illustration of a married couple who have come for counseling. Notice the linguistic patterns being used by the couple as they try to describe the "problem."

Let us imagine that the well-intentioned counselor decides to respond to the above situation by turning to the woman and saying, "It's obvious that you are upset. What are your feelings telling you? Speak from your guts; share your emotions with us." In this hypothetical example, the woman might reply with: "Well, I don't really know what you mean. It just seems that everything I do is wrong. Things just aren't what I pictured they would be when I got married, and my husband doesn't even seem to care."

The key to this fictional interaction is in the woman's response to the counselor. She is being very honest with him when she says she really doesn't know what he means. For him to persist in asking her to "contact those feelings" or to "get in touch with her emotions" may lead to a counterproductive session. This is a situation where using the same "language" as the client could prove invaluable. Once he gains rapport with the woman, once she has the sense that he really "understands" her, then he can begin to systematically alter his language, "translating" the language of one system into another in order to effectively communicate with both her and her husband. The next step is to *teach* the couple to speak and understand each other's language. This can be done either overtly by talking about the use of predicates or through example by simply continuing to "translate" whenever appropriate.

Functional Differences

It is perhaps the "mismatching" of predicates that accounts in part for the confounding fact that "great" therapists can work miracles with some clients but are almost totally ineffective with others. Preferred representational systems may also play an important role in a therapist's choice of which psychotherapeutic techniques to study. For example, the more traditional psychotherapies rely heavily on the client's ability to digitalize – to talk about – and to visualize various experiences. Some of the humanistic approaches, on the other hand, identify feelings or emotions as the medium through which to achieve change. These are *functional differences* – differences that, on the positive side, enable individuals with different models of the world to seek out and work within a system that best suits their own.

The sooner you begin to match the client's predicates, to speak his own language, the more rapidly therapy can progress. This is true in any situation where a close relationship is being fostered, whether you are a therapist, a teacher, an office manager, or a coach. The ability to adapt your own language to the predicates of others is as important in a close intimate relationship like a family as it is in situations where people must work together. The following illustration demonstrates what sometimes happens when two people who come together in the work environment speak two different "languages."

The result of changing your language to match the person you are talking with is two-fold. First, the person begins to feel more at ease with you and is more likely to trust you: "Ah! Someone who really understands me!" Second, you create an environment in which miscommunication is much less likely to occur. This is because you leave no room for contradictions between what you say or ask for and the internal experience – model of the world – of the person you are talking with. Also, because you are more "like" him in his experience, it is easier for him to "like" you.

Representational System Hierarchies

A person's preferred representational system is the one in which he generally makes the most number of distinctions about the world. One way to determine which system a person prefers is to give him the Representational System Bias Test (see Appendix B). By tallying the scores as shown, you can determine a person's *representational system hierarchy*.[6] His preferred system will have a higher score than his *secondary system* and so on. This "ranking" of a person's representational systems has some important ramifications. As demonstrated in previous examples, difficulties can arise when two people who need to communicate each have different preferred systems. This is especially true when the difference between the scores is large as in the example below.

Person A: V - 7   K - 20   A - 10   D - 13

Person B: V - 20   K - 6   A - 9   D - 15

Person A's *least* valued system (the visual system) is person B's *preferred* system and vice versa. In terms of being able to "speak the same language," their representational system hierarchies already pose a formidable obstacle to effective communication!

The Communication Categories Model

Predicate preference is only one indication of how people are representing or experiencing the world. In this section we will explore other ways people indicate their preferred systems, many of which can be observed before they even open their mouths.

Caution: Generalization Ahead

In the discussion about human modeling processes in Chapter 1, one of the primary areas we focused on was *generalization*, which is important to our ability to learn a great complexity of information and new behaviors. However, generalizations may also become a source of pain for an individual by limiting both behavior and perception in non-productive ways.

The Meta principles of communication and change presented in this handbook are based on generalizations – behavioral patterns within an individual's sphere of activity as well as consistencies of interaction between members of a society. But these are only generalizations; they are only *models* of behavior.

It is important to remember a point made earlier: everyone has a different map or model of reality. *We are all different*. What is presented on the following pages are generalizations about people that are only useful when they assist us in more efficient and effective communication. *Be wary* of the potential to become limited by these same generalizations. It is better to trust what you see, hear, and feel than to rely on a highly generalized model of behavior. Please remember: if the model doesn't fit, *don't use it*.

Based in part on the work of family therapist Virginia Satir[7] and the human behavior modelers Bandler and Grinder,[8] we have consolidated into a model four basic *communication categories*. This model is organized around the four preferred representational systems. These are the visual system, the kinesthetic system, the auditory–tonal system, and the digital system.

There is an efficient shorthand that will be used throughout this book to identify each of the communication categories. Because the model is organized around the four representational systems, the following labels will be used. A person demonstrating characteristics associated with the visual communication category will be called a "visual." One who is operating within the kinesthetic modality will be called a "kino." Someone exhibiting behaviors associated with the auditory system will be called a "tonal," and a person operating out of the digital system will be called a "digital."

These labels can be used in two ways. One way is to describe an individual who habitually represents experience with one of the systems more often than the others. The other way is to describe how an individual is representing his experience in a particular situation. In this case, the label identifies the *dominant* mode of behavior in that particular situation. In the illustration on page 52, for example, we could say that the man is *being* a "kino," and the woman is *being* a "visual."

The following list represents the specific areas of behavior covered by the communication categories model. These behaviors are different for each of the four systems and are described in detail in the text. A complete chart with specific behaviors listed under the "visual," "kino," "tonal, and "digital" systems is presented in Appendix C.[9]

1. Predicates that presuppose a representational system (preferred system)

2. Postural characteristics

3. Body "types" and movements

4. Lip size

5. Breathing patterns

6. Voice tonality, speed, and tempo

7. Eye elevation in relation to others

8. Rules for looking while listening

9. Satir categories

10. Meta Model violations: linguistic idiosyncrasies

11. Meta Model ill-formed meanings

12. Accessing cues

It is important to keep in mind throughout this book the warning previously issued. This model and the labels associated with it are only generalizations about people. They delete a great deal of information; this is a part of how they are supposed to function. They can make it easier for us to perceive, understand, and predict behavior. However, as mentioned in a popular text on psychology, "Labels intended to be merely descriptive may also come to be regarded as explanations of the problem" (Coleman, 1972, p. 642). They should never be used in a way that might interfere with either our *perceptions of* or our *behaviors toward* those we have labeled. The examples that follow are intended to simplify the task of detecting behavioral patterns. However, remember that it is always best to use your own observations when a model doesn't fit.

Posture and Body Cues

Although heredity plays an important part in creating the physical appearance we each display, psychologists have long recognized the relationship between personality – our model of the world – and physical characteristics.[10] Because these physical qualities are externally exhibited, they are communicative signals that can be useful tools in the process of demystifying communication.

"Visuals"

"Mrs. McCulvary was my third grade teacher. We remember her well if not fondly. She was so skinny and tall, our nickname for her was 'ostrich,' although that could also be because of the colorful 'plumage' she sometimes wore. She always seemed to look down her nose at everyone, and she had a tendency to screech whenever she talked to us."

The above description of the fictional Mrs. McCulvary is a good example of some of the characteristics often displayed by "visuals." It is not unusual for the habitual "visual" to be thin, although you will occasionally run across a very fat or obese "visual" (see "Body: Brief Analysis" box below). They usually stand erect with their shoulders held up or back. People who are behaving as a "visual" will keep their necks straight and erect, matching their bodies. They often appear to "lead with their chin" when they walk, and their motions can be described as stiff or jerky. Habitual "visuals" will often have a smaller rib extension than individuals from the other categories, and they tend to breathe more into the upper portion of the chest. It is not uncommon for the "visual" to speak in a fast, clear, or distinct way with a higher pitch than people operating from the other categories.

The following illustration shows some of the physical characteristics described above. Some of these postural and tonal behaviors can be observed in individuals operating out of the visual system even though their preferred system is not visual. This would include breathing and movement, although the visual body type and rib cage extension would most likely be demonstrated only by a habitual "visual." *This ability to operate in systems other than the preferred system is true for all of the communication categories.*

Visual

"Kinos"

Think of the image evoked by Santa Claus. He is always depicted as a soft and rather round man with rosy cheeks and a flowing white beard. When he laughs, his whole belly jiggles, and the feelings he elicits are warm and happy.

The figure of Santa is an appropriate example of a "kino." The habitual "kino" generally has more flesh on his body than individuals from the other categories, although they tend not to be obese. When communicating from this modality, individuals will often demonstrate a rounding of the shoulders, and they sometimes bend slightly forward as they speak and listen. Their motions tend to be flowing and loose; how else would Santa get down the chimney! Habitual "kinos" often have a larger rib extension compared to the other categories. When operating from this modality, people tend to breathe into the lower portion of the lungs. The tonality of a "kino" might be generalized as having soft or airy qualities with a slower tempo and lower tone and volume than the other categories. The illustration below represents some of the qualities typical of these individuals.

Kino

Body: Brief Analysis

If you think in terms of the aspect of experience the habitual "kino" or "visual" is paying attention to, the structure of their bodies begins to make sense. When operating from the visual modality, a person becomes *dissociated* or disconnected from bodily experiences. This is because it is primarily the visual portions of the environment that command his attention. Physical demands such as hunger (or fullness!) often go unnoticed and, though habitual "visuals" tend to be slimmer than people whose preferred system is kinesthetic, they can also become obese. Unlike the "visuals," habitual "kinos" are more alert to bodily needs and comforts, including hunger and eating, so their frames tend to fill out. Also, where a "visual" will wear sharp, well-coordinated, and tailored clothing, a "kino" is more likely to wear soft and comfortable knits and fabrics.

Again, these are generalizations. We all have the ability to "be" any of the communication categories at different times. What is offered here are patterns of observable behavior, consistencies from which we can effectively predict specific styles of communication and portions of experience people are likely to be most aware of.

"Tonals"

It appears that, at least in the United States and other Western cultures, the proportion of habitual "tonals" is small in relation to the other categories. Because of this, it is more difficult to make accurate generalizations about them. Our experience with the few we have met leads us to believe that their physiques vary but tend toward the slim rather than the obese. A common communicative posture for this group, as shown below, is having the arms folded across the chest with the head tilted down and to the side, perhaps to listen. When they speak, they maintain more control over the auditory portion of communication than most people. In order to maintain this control over their reproduction of tonal aspects of their speech, they need to have a full range of breathing. They tend, therefore, to have larger rib cages than "visuals" and to utilize their lungs more fully.

Tonal

"Digitals"

A person who is communicating from the digital modality generally speaks in a clipped, crisp monotone. Since variations in tone are relatively unimportant to them, the habitual "digital" exhibits breathing patterns more like those of a "visual," that is, higher up in the chest. The digital system is based on language, a behavior that is acquired as a person matures. A "digital" person, like a "visual," is dissociated from his feelings. Since faculty with language comes somewhat later in life than visual, tonal, and kinesthetic abilities, it may be that a person becomes "digitalized" in response to some environmental situation. Most "digitals" that we have observed have physical body types similar to a "kino." This suggests the adoption of the digital system as a means of coping (through dissociation) with feelings that may not be pleasant. The following image illustrates some of the qualities of a "digital."

Digital

Lip Size

One interesting characteristic that seems to correlate with a person's communication category is the size of the lips. This is especially true of the lower lip. You may find it interesting to match this phenomenon with your own observations. Visually oriented persons are often characterized by rather thin, tight lips. People operating out of the kinesthetic category usually demonstrate fuller, softer lips. "Tonals" and "digitals" vary, however, the latter tending more toward thinner and tighter lips.

Voice: Brief Analysis

Characteristics of voice associated with each of the communication categories are related to breathing patterns. For example, where "visuals" tend to breathe higher up in the chest, it makes sense that the volume of air taken in will be less than that taken in by a "tonal" who utilizes more of the lungs. With so much less volume, the "visual" needs to speak faster in order to say as much with each breath. It may be that they often talk with a higher pitched voice because this cuts off more of the flow of air crossing the vocal chords, enabling them to conserve air.

"Kinos," on the other hand, in order to breathe as deeply as they do, must open up the windpipe more. This can give their voices a more breathy or airy quality when they speak. This relaxation of the throat may also add to the tendency to speak at a slower pace than the other categories.

Remember, we all have the ability to "be" any one or even a combination of each of these categories at different times. Even the habitual "visual," "kino," "tonal," and "digital" can fluctuate, making body type or build unreliable. Rather than depending on a highly generalized model, it is always better to maintain open and clear perceptual channels and trust your own *experience*.

Other Behavioral Cues

There are certain patterns of behavior that seem to be consistent within each of the communication categories, particularly in stressful situations. A person who is *being* "visual" pays most attention to the visual aspects of an interaction. This includes both the facial expressions and other gestures and movements of those around him as well as his own internally generated visual imagery. In order to adequately attend to someone he is talking to, it is important for the "visual" to situate himself so that he can clearly see as much of that person as possible. Because of this, "visuals" tend to keep more physical distance between themselves and others, at least enough to be able to see most, if not all, of those with whom they are communicating. Because they often place themselves at an angle that will give them the best vantage point, usually somewhat above others, they often appear to be "looking down on" everyone else.

People who are operating out of the kinesthetic communication category rely heavily on feelings in order to understand and make sense out of what is happening around them. They are most likely to place themselves, whenever possible, in a position in which they can be close enough to actually touch the people they are talking with. Just as the "visual" gains information about a speaker by observing subtle movements, muscular tension and relaxation, the "kino" gains the same information through touch and close proximity. Though people operating out of either of these systems have the ability to use any representational system, they will tend to rely upon their preferred system for most of their information.

As you can imagine, there is great potential for discomfort and miscommunication between individuals communicating from these two different communication categories. Where the "visual" needs distance so as to get a "clear picture" of the process, the "kino" wants to get close enough to insure a "good connection." However, the moment the "kino" pushes past the comfortable distance range for the "visual," the "visual" goes into stress. This stress is communicated – usually analogically through a tightening of the skeletal muscles and a strain in the voice tonality – to the "kino" who responds by also going into stress. Of course, in the stress situation, the "kino" will want even more "contact," and the demands for closeness increase resulting in even more stress for the "visual."

The processes described above all go on almost totally outside the awareness of the individuals involved. This is a common pattern found in couples who come in for counseling. The results are often verbalized in the following way:

Husband: I never feel as if we have really connected, especially when
             we argue. I feel like there's a great distance between us.

Wife: He never seems to get the whole picture. He's always invading my space and "pawing" at me while we're trying to have a serious conversation.

(Of course, these roles are just as often reversed.)

Anthropologist Edward Hall has noticed similar patterns within whole cultures. In an interview with Kenneth Friedman, Hall points out that of the cultures he has studied, the Arabs prefer a much closer "conversational distance" than any of the others, especially compared to the typical American. His description of their behaviors is an interesting blend of social constraints (see Chapter 1) and representational systems:

Overall, what they're doing is coding, sort of synthesizing, their reactions. They say to themselves, "How do I feel about this person?" In contemporary American terms: "What kind of vibes am I getting from him?" They are also responding to smell and to the thermal qualities of the other person. We talk about someone with a warm personality. This is literally true, and there is [also] a very cold fish. This is the person who draws heat from you. So they're picking up thermal, olfactory, and kinesthetic cues also. A lot of touching goes on during conversations in the Middle East ... (Friedman, 1979, p. 48)

General positioning in relation to others for "tonals" and "digitals" is less consistent, though they will both tend to place themselves close enough to hear. Also, for "digitals" both physical and eye contact are avoided. It may be that visual input distracts the "digital" from the high concentration necessary to maintain control over his verbal output, while a touch has the potential to "reconnect" him with the feelings from which he is dissociated. Where "digitals" and "visuals" will gaze above the heads of others – "thinking" and "searching for the correct words to say" – "tonals" tend to avert their eyes down and away from the speaker, also in order to keep from being distracted, though more often during listening than speaking.

Touching

Those who habitually communicate from the digital category can be thought of as having learned a particular coping pattern. Especially under stress, these individuals appear to *dissociate* from their feelings, emotions, and even from an awareness of the body. They do this by "going into their heads" and filling the void with a flood of words.

Touching people who are behaving in this manner, who are communicating from this category, may suddenly remind them of their bodies and of the feelings and emotions from which they have dissociated themselves. It may be for this reason that they have learned to keep some physical distance between themselves and others. This is an important point to remember when communicating with "digitals," and in some cases with "visuals" as well. A touch can be utilized to distract these individuals from their ongoing thought processes. Touching can also be used to assist them in reconnecting with their bodies and emotions.

Rules for Listening

There appear to be certain rules for listening associated with each of the communication categories. Though these rules vary from one culture to another, for each category they remain consistent within the culture.[11] The rules regard direct eye contact and are described below. Once learned, these rules can provide you with more understanding of and control over the communication process.

A person operating out of the visual system must be able to *see* the speaker in order to easily understand what is being said. This need is then generalized or "projected" onto others with whom the "visual" is communicating. The *look-to-listen* rule can be stated as follows:

> Since I must look at you in order to hear and understand you, then you must look at me in order for me to know that you are hearing and understanding me.

Note the how the rule represents a special type of *complex equivalence*. This will be covered in greater detail in Chapter 3. In the case of "digitals," and especially with "tonals," the look-to-listen rule is reversed as *the must-look-away* rule. Since visual input is a distraction to their ability to hear and understand, "tonals" and "digitals" might state the looking rule as follows:

I must look away in order to hear and understand.

This rule is not projected onto others, however, like the look-to-listen rule of the "visuals." The "tonal" and "digital" do not need to look to see whether or not the person listening is looking, since the visual component is not the important element for them in the communication process.

The contradiction between the two rules for listening has many ramifications. How often have you encountered or participated in the scene illustrated below in which the angry adult takes the child's chin in hand, saying, "Look at me when I'm talking to you"? This could be an example of conflict between the look-to-listen and must-look-away rules.

Look-to-listen rule

In stressful situations, "digitals" and "tonals" are usually less comfortable trying to understand what is being said to them if they are being "forced" to make eye contact. This is also generally true for someone operating out of the kinesthetic model. What these people see distracts their attention from the representational system in which they make the most distinctions. The other systems simply fail to provide information in ways that are as easily utilized by them as the information that matches their preferred system.

There is another difficulty that arises when someone with the look-to-listen rule also believes that if someone looks away while speaking, it means that he is lying.[12] In the situation illustrated above, if the child is not operating out of the visual system, he may find it difficult to talk while looking directly at the adult. Again, due to the visual distraction, the child might have trouble "thinking" in his habitual system without looking away. This could create dire consequences if the adult thinks the child is lying because he keeps looking away.

In Chapter 1 a somewhat different eye contact rule was discussed regarding social constraints (see page 23). In that example, it was demonstrated how a lack of knowledge or understanding of the social rule governing direct eye contact could lead to conflict between individuals from different cultural backgrounds. It is important to recognize that differences also exist between individuals in a homogeneous social group. This is because people tend to orient themselves to aspects of experience that correlate to their preferred representational systems. When you can identify these differences between people, you can more easily "tune in to," "see clearly," and "connect" with other people's models of the world. This is one of those "magical" qualities of very effective communicators. By identifying and then using these differences, you will run less of a risk of making the mistake of judging another's behavior solely by the standards of your own model. You can more easily "bridge the gap" between yourself and your clients, students, co-workers, and anyone else with whom it is important for you to communicate.

Satir Categories

The following behavioral patterns come from an unusually gifted people helper, Virginia Satir. In her book, *Peoplemaking*, she identifies five "postural stances" that people take during the communication process.[13] Of the five stances, only one represents *congruent* communication: the "levelling" response occurs during communication when "all parts of the message are going in the same direction – the voice says words that match the facial expression, the body position, and the voice tone" (p. 72). In their exaggerated form, says Satir, "so exaggerated that nobody could miss it" (p. 63), we have incorporated the remaining four into our communications categories model as the "Satir Categories," so called after the work of Bandler and Grinder.[14] These postures are associated with the communication categories as follows.

Under stress, "visuals" tend to take on the postural characteristics of Satir's "blamer." That is, they take on an aggressive stance, pointing their fingers at the person they are talking to and using expressions like: "You always do that. Why can't you do anything right?" (A more complete presentation of word-patterns used by each of the communication categories is presented in the next chapter.)

People who are operating as "kinos" assume the "placater" stance, especially under stress. Satir pictures a person down on one knee, hands turned palms-up as if "begging for forgiveness." Phrases associated with this posture are: "I feel so bad about making you mad at me. I just can't do anything right. Please forgive me."

"Digitals" take the "computer" posture. Crossing their arms and avoiding eye contact by looking over everyone's head, it is easy to become lost in their super-logical, non-sensory-based language. Again, particularly in stressful situations, these individuals use expressions like: "The correct procedure in such cases, especially if one concurs with the current arguments, might be suggested as being statistically more appropriate to the former rather than the latter remarks."

Although the "tonal" person sometimes takes on "computer" characteristics, he is more likely to assume the role of Satir's "distracter." If he overhears two people talking who are just on the verge of getting angry (remember, he is extremely sensitive to their tonal cues, so his "timing" is exquisite!), he may suddenly interrupt them by asking for the time of day, by turning on the TV or radio too loud, or by some other distracting action. Under stress, as in the above situation, the "tonal" is likely to say such things as, "It's good that people like you can keep such a harmonious relationship. It must be nice to know you're being thought of. Where's the TV guide?"

Satir points out that there is often a difference between what the person's body appears to communicate and what is actually "going on inside." Where the "computer" stance seems to express "calm, cool, and collected," says Satir, this person may actually be feeling very vulnerable. The "placater" says "I'm helpless" with his posture while inside he is feeling completely worthless. The "blamer" who is communicating "I am the boss around here" with his stance is feeling lonely and unsuccessful, while the constantly irrelevant "distracter" with his unbalanced stance may be feeling that nobody cares.

Each of the Satir stances can also be exhibited in less obvious ways. Hand gestures often indicate one of the postures. The pointing of a finger or an upturned hand may indicate blaming and placating postures respectively. Especially when combined with key phrases like "You always ..." and "I'm sorry ..." these gestures can be important indications about how a person is relating to the world and to others around him. Detection of such patterns can assist you in gaining rapport with the people you live and work with while aiding you in understanding how people get "stuck" in communicative patterns that consistently fail to give them what they want and need.

Another Warning

The previous generalizations are not to be considered universally applicable. They are presented as useful tools for noticing and describing patterns in people's behavior. We teach these tools to help the student of this model become more sensitive to and aware of what is being presented to them by the person with whom they are communicating; to become more externally oriented, rather than attending to their own personal model of the world. When a behavior is identified as fitting in with several other patterns, it can be used to help you understand that person's model of the world and can assist you in gaining the trust and rapport necessary for effective communication. These generalizations are only models and as such contain all the limitations inherent in any model. *Use them when and where they apply, and discard them whenever they don't fit.*

Summary

In this chapter, stress was mentioned in relation to a person's preferred representational system. What makes it so important is the effect it has on an individual's perceptions and behavior. As demonstrated with the story about the panic-stricken man, individuals under stress tend to turn to the representational system in which they make the most distinctions. This *coping* behavior, likely learned early in life, proved itself useful in enough situations to warrant its being maintained. The insidious thing about this kind of strategy for coping is that it is during stressful situations that people should have the greatest number of distinctions and as much information about their environment as possible. Ironically, it is during these very times of need that people tend to choose (unconsciously) to adopt the limiting patterns of their preferred systems, often to the exclusion of the other systems.

When people walk into a therapist's office for counseling, it is usually because they have only very limited resources at their disposal. People often seek counseling because they are suffering the stresses associated with emotional pain or with the problems of dealing with a complex society. Recognizing people's limitations can be the first step in assisting them in discovering alternatives, new choices of perception and behavior. This is true in many different settings, from the classroom to the business office.

Your ability to identify and use the same representational system being used by those you work and live with will assist you in developing and maintaining a high level of effective communication. Determining the communication categories that these people use in various situations can help you gain their trust while enabling you to obtain the information necessary in order to assist them in making changes they want and need. This is truly the "magic" of powerful and effective communication.

When a person communicates with you, he presents you with information about how he has created his model of the world. This includes data about how and where some of the limits were built into his model. With this information, you are not only able to *pace* his experience (gain/maintain rapport), you are also able to *lead* him in changing his perceptions and behaviors that are limiting and painful. This can be done verbally as well as non-verbally by utilizing all the analog systems of body posture, breathing, voice tonality, and so on. The example that follows will demonstrate some of these techniques.

A highly visual person has come in for an initial interview. You know this from a combination of body posturing, build, lip size, clothing, predicate usage, and other cues. You already know that one of his rules for communicating is that it is necessary to look in order to understand what another person is saying. If you were to turn away or listen by diverting your head, as some people do, he might accuse you of not paying attention. This poor pace could be compounded further if you placed yourself too close and "invaded his space." Remember that visually oriented people are generally more comfortable when they can see you from a distance in order to get "the whole perspective."

By accepting this person's rules, by matching his predicates – in essence, by operating out of his model of the world – you begin to pave the road for a successful relationship. You can *mirror* various aspects of this person's communication category by matching your body posture, tonality, predicates, and by obeying the rules associated with that system. This will sometimes enable you to detect areas of pain and limits to this person's perception that would otherwise have remained hidden from you. At the same time you demonstrate "acceptance" by mirroring, you provide the person with the opportunity to *see*, *hear*, and *feel* himself in ways which are usually outside of his conscious awareness. As long as the rapport is maintained, you can utilize this subtle form of *feedback*. For example, you can lead the person to a more comfortable or functional place by simply *modeling* those changes in yourself. By changing his "reflection" in this way, the person has the opportunity to actually experience new choices at a deep, unconscious level, to "try them on" so to speak. As long as you are open to subtle changes in the person you are working with, you can immediately tell whether or not the changes are appropriate for him.

These are just a few of the ways in which this information can be utilized. As you learn and experience the subtle patterns of communication covered in this book, you may find yourself generating more and more innovative applications in many different situations.

A complete chart of all the behavioral characteristics associated with each of the communication categories is provided in Appendix C.

Notes to Chapter 2

1. The term "representational system" comes from Bandler and Grinder. For additional information, see Bandler and Grinder (1975, pp. 6–26).

2. In keeping with the Bandler and Grinder model, we have put the olfactory and gustatory systems together. The name "olfactory" and symbol "O" are used because we make so many more distinctions with our sense of smell than with our sense of taste, which can only differentiate between four basic stimuli: sweet, sour, salty, and bitter.

3. Bandler and Grinder (1976) discuss "the most highly valued representational system" (p. 8). They expand on this later: "By most highly valued representational system we mean the ... system the person typically uses to bring information into consciousness," and "no special one of the ... systems is better than the others, although some may be more efficient for certain tasks" (p. 26). We have incorporated this construct into the preferred representational system (PRS) in its greatly expanded form as presented in this book. We should point out, however, that the research on PRS has been inconclusive. As previously mentioned, one writer has gone so far as to state: "there is not ... any substance to the conjecture that people represent their world internally in a preferred mode which may be inferred from their choice of predicates" (Heap, 1988, p. 275), although his findings have been questioned by others such as Tosey and Mathison (2009), who suggest his conclusion should be qualified by the number (too few) and quality (a majority were postgraduate dissertations) of the studies reviewed by Heap (p. 134).

4. Unlike information entering our brains from the other sensory systems, smell does not pass through the thalamus and, therefore, is not subjected to the thalamic filtering that other systems undergo.

5. See the section "Trust: Gaining Rapport" in Chapter 1.

6. For more information, see the section "Mapping" in Chapter 4.

7. Especially important is Satir's book *Peoplemaking* (1972) which will be referred to later in this section.

8. Bandler and Grinder's two books, *The Structure of Magic, Vol. I* (1975) and *Vol. II* (1976), contain some of the information used to create the communication categories model presented in this book.

9. This chart was developed primarily through the work of Frank Pucelik of the Meta Institute with input from students in various parts of the United States. It would be interesting to compare these observations with those of individuals from other cultural backgrounds.

10. William Sheldon, author of *The Varieties of Human Physique* (1940) and *The Varieties of Human Temperament* (1942), is famous for his research on the relationship between temperament and physique. Although this book presents correlations between various patterns of behavior, including body types, the need for further research poses exciting possibilities to experimental psychologists and others in the field of human communications.

11. See the section "Constraints on the Model" in Chapter 1, especially "Social Constraints."

12. This is another example of a complex equivalence (see pages 31–32 and 118–119). In this case, a particular meaning, "lying," is attached to a specific behavior – looking away while talking. Thus, a behavior that is necessary to the person who needs to look away while talking can pose problems if it is misinterpreted by someone with the above complex equivalence. There is an excellent discussion of complex equivalence in Bandler et al. (1976), beginning on p. 38.

13. See Satir (1972, pp. 59–85) for a complete presentation of her "patterns of communication."

14. See Bandler and Grinder (1976, p. 47).

Chapter 3
The Meta Model

If he is indeed wise [the teacher] does not bid you enter the house of his wisdom, but rather leads you to the threshold of your own mind.

Kahlil Gibran, *The Prophet*

The Digital Representational System

Symbolic Representation

The digital system, language, is the *symbolic* representation of experience. It is the only system that can represent all the other representational systems as well as being able to represent itself. Not directly related to any of our sensory organs, it is so unique that it warrants special attention. The historical importance of this system is discussed by Mike and Nancy Samuels in their book *Seeing with the Mind's Eye*. As they put it:

> With the development of language and a written system for recording it, rational thought came to dominate. Words came to function as labels, allowing man to detach himself from his experience and analyze it ...

> With these changes came the birth of civilization, law and order, the development of philosophical and moral systems and the growth of mathematics and the sciences. As knowledge and communication increased, people began to live out highly specialized social roles, carrying the sense of separation and alienation from nature to its extreme. (1975, pp. 12–13)

Such a powerful tool, the digital system! As with the other systems, it is not only an indicator of how a person creates his model of the world, but it also serves to enhance as well as limit perception. The discussion of social

77

constraints (Chapter 1) described how our ability to name something affects how we perceive it. In one example, the Eskimos' ability to name over seventy different kinds of snow was shown to be very important to their survival in the harsh northern climates. Only with their specific linguistic (digital) background is it possible to perceive the variations in the quality of snow indicated by their vocabulary.

Built into the encoding element of our linguistic processes is what we might call a *perceptual enhancer*. Once a linguistic symbol has been assigned to a specific experience, it becomes a discrete, manipulable element that is differentiated from the surrounding environment or experience. The powerful effect of language is discussed by the general semanticist J. Samuel Bois in his book *The Art of Awareness*. He says:

> We see the world through the meshes of that human-made filter; we project on the world of phenomena the relations that we have learned to observe among the parts of speech; we interpret what is happening in terms of the logic of cause–effect that is embedded in our grammar. (1966, p. 19)

Analog vs. Digital Communication

The key to digital expression (language) is the *arbitrary* assignment of word-symbols to things or processes. There is no necessary connection between the name and the thing named. On the contrary, analog, by definition, means that something is similar to something else. Therefore, we can expect that analogic "language" or communication will more closely relate to what it is about.

For example, if we hear the word "eat" in an unfamiliar language, we are not likely to understand it. It is merely an arbitrarily assigned (digital) symbol for a common behavior. If, however, the person pantomimes the behavior (eating), that is, uses analogic communication, the meaning is much more likely to be understood.

But where analogic communication is more universal (and more "primitive"[1]), it is also limited in some very important ways. Since analogic communication can only portray a thing or an action, it cannot portray a thought or idea and is therefore unable to portray negation. Only the more abstract and versatile digital representation system can express negation.

The digital system can also convey time and number manipulations that analog systems cannot.

Another limitation is that of ambiguity. A smile (analog) can come from an experience of pleasure or an experience of pain ("Grin and bear it"). A shrug of the shoulders can mean "I give up," "I don't care," or "I don't know." With analog communications, there is always the risk of error in translation, and in human analog systems there are no qualifiers to indicate which message is implied.[2]

By understanding the value of the mechanisms involved in the process of affixing labels to our experiences, we can become more alert to some of the effects these labels have on our perception. It is not unusual to judge behavior by its appearance, attaching a name or label to it and more or less "reifying" it. This tends to halt or at least limit future observations of the behavior's *effects*. Mara Palazzoli and her team of researchers discuss this problem in their book *Paradox and Counterparadox*. What they discovered working with schizophrenic families was that *appearance* is not necessarily a valid indication of the *meaning* of a behavior. They write: "For example, if a patient appeared to be sad, we concluded he *was* sad, and we went so far as to try to understand *why* he was sad, inviting and encouraging him to speak to us about his sadness" (1978, p. 26).

Linguistic Deconditioning

Taking their understanding one step further, Palazzoli and her colleagues began to explore the *function* of the client's behavior not only within the family system but also with the therapists themselves. Through a process they call "linguistic deconditioning," they began to change their perception of the client's behavior from one of *being*, as in "He is (being) sad," to one of *seeming* or *showing*, as in "He is showing sadness" or "He seems sad."

From this vantage point, it is much easier to observe the *effects* of the behavior rather than to dwell on the *causes* of the behavior. It can be much more useful to define the meaning of a behavior or communication by its ultimate effects on those around the communicator. This is especially important with some forms of analog communication.

The Meta Model: Overview

In 1975 Richard Bandler and John Grinder published a book that outlined their now popular Meta Model: *The Structure of Magic, Vol. I*.[3] This is a linguistic (digital) tool which has proven extremely useful in therapeutic as well as other settings. It is based on the observation that human behavior, especially linguistic behavior, is rule governed. The same processes of generalization, deletion, and distortion used in creating our models of reality are also used in the creation of our linguistic representations of experience.

L. Michael Hall (unless otherwise noted, all citations attributed to Hall in this chapter come from his book, *Communication Magic*, 2001) observed that the original presentation of the Meta Model in Bandler and Grinder's *The Structure of Magic* was "without form. The ideas were there, the terminology was there, but it was structureless. It appeared first in no sequential or orderly form ... the ideas lacked a user-friendly form" (p. 149). One of the major contributions made by one of the authors of this book (Frank Pucelik) was to organize the model as it is presented here. This, by the way, was in great part the inspiration behind the use of the word *demystified* in the title of this work, because this well-organized presentation makes it so much more *accessible*.

As it is presented here, the Meta Model includes several distinctions not in the original, and the format has been altered. The basic assumptions still apply however. Since it is a linguistic tool, the Meta Model relies on the natural intuitions of any native speaker of the English language.[4] We would like to point out also that the model that follows has been expanded to include Hall's unique contribution of nine new distinctions. We will refer to the summary of Hall's version of the Meta Model (see Appendix D) regularly throughout this chapter, because it is a version regularly being taught in Neuro-Linguistic Programming seminars and courses.

Transformational Grammar

At the time of this book's original publication, a contemporary school of linguistics[5] proposed a relationship between what is spoken or written by an individual and a deeper internal linguistic representation. Still a useful model of language, Transformational Grammar calls the production of a sentence, the actual sound or written sequence of symbols and phrases, the surface structure (SS). The deep structure (DS) is also a system of symbols and phrases, but it is much more complex and abstract. The DS is the complete linguistic representation of a person's experience that might be considered the intent or the thought behind the SS sentence.

The theory is that the DS is transformed into SS by a series of rules. Transformational grammarians say that the DS and the SS are related by certain formal operations that conform to the concepts of generalizations, deletion, and distortion covered in Chapter 1.

Of note, Hall points out that, while transformational grammar formed the basis for Bandler and Grinder's original Meta Model, shortly after their book was published, linguists including Noam Chomsky had abandoned it and moved on to other linguistic models such as Generative Semantics. Hall based his own work in part on Korzybski's General Semantics epistemological model which he says "provides a much fuller and more accurate paradigm for the Meta-Model" (p. 293). He goes on to say that, like General Semantics, the Meta Model "focuses primarily on identifying poor mapping (ill-formedness) that prevents full and resourceful living ... As a neuro-linguistic model, it seeks to identify expressions that mark our problem areas in mapping (in one's schema or model of the world) that affect psychological functioning (how we think, feel, speak, behave, relate, etc.)" (p. 295).

In any communication, the spoken or written language (SS) provides the listener with a rich variety of information about the speaker. It indicates how that person makes sense of the world, how he distorts his perceptions, and when and where those distortions occur. Predicates, for example, may indicate his preferred representational system. The surface structure can also indicate when and what kinds of experiences the speaker systematically leaves out of his representation of the world. By assisting the speaker in "reconnecting" with the unspoken portion of his digital representation of experience (DS) you begin a process of exploration. This process can fill in gaps of understanding that may occur between you and assist the speaker in recognizing and confronting limitations to growth and experience he may not even have known existed.

Meta Model Violations

Any time you are reading or listening to a person speak and you find your-self having to "go inside" to understand what is being said, it is a pretty good indication that you have experienced what is called a "Meta Model violation." The fact that you are confused or that you need to internally generate information that is missing from or distorted in the speaker's SS is a cue that your intuitive processes as a native speaker are being utilized. This is a valuable process because it allows the speaker/writer to share a great deal of information rapidly without needing to fill in all the missing pieces. However, the same process may drastically limit the speaker's abil-ity to express what he really means. A person's language can also indicate areas where he has limits on his ability to perceive the full richness of certain experiences. The result of such limitations and distortions may be that the speaker has few choices about how to feel or behave in certain situations.

Meta Model Responses

What the Meta Model does is make explicit those semantic and syntac-tic contexts, those expressions in which Meta Model violations occur. Once they can be systematically recognized, there are specific Meta Model responses that you can use to recover deleted material and to assist the speaker in reconnecting with his deep structure. Reconnecting with the fullest linguistic representation of a person's experience can aid him in understanding how certain generalizations, deletions, and distortions cause pain and limit choice and perception. This paves the way for healthy growth and positive change.

The Meta Model as originally presented in this chapter is a set of nine[6] linguistic distinctions that can be grouped into three categories. The first category, *gathering information*, begins the process of uncovering and exploring specific portions of the speaker's experience that are missing from his surface structure or that are presented in a distorted form. The second category, *expanding limits*, provides you with tools to assist the speaker in defining and then expanding the boundaries or limitations of his model of the world. This self-exploration assists the speaker in gaining more choices in both behavior and perception. The final category, *chang-ing meanings*, continues the process of growth and expansion by exploring with the speaker how he understands himself and his relationship with the people around him and with the world in general. With this revised edition, we have included an additional category, expanding the model with nine new distinctions identified by Hall (2001).

Meta Model Diagram #1

The deep structure is the most complete linguistic representation that a person could give to experience. This is symbolized by the larger form below. The deep structure includes the boundary line and all the space contained within it.

The surface structure is the portion of the deep structure expressed by an individual when he speaks or writes. It is represented by the smaller shape that lies within the larger form. Notice in the illustration below how the "shape" of the SS conforms to the "shape" of the DS. Since the transformational processes of creating the SS from the DS are essentially the same as the processes we use to create our models of reality, the SS is an invaluable indicator of how the speaker perceives the world around him. It is through the SS that we gain clues about the rest of the speaker's model. With the aid of the first category of Meta Model responses to violations, we gain more information about the larger portion of the model below, the DS.

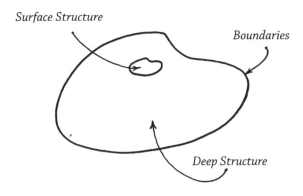

Surface Structure

Boundaries

Deep Structure

We highly recommend that anyone learning the Meta Model read this chapter carefully in order to get the general feel and logic of the model.

Then go back to the beginning and start with the first distinction. Attuning yourself to each distinction, hearing it when it comes up, and being able to respond with the appropriate Meta Model response smoothly and naturally usually takes about one week. Then you can easily go on to the next distinction, knowing that the first has become a comfortable, functional habit. Doing this with each distinction will enable you to rapidly and easily incorporate the Meta Model as an exceptionally powerful communication tool.[7]

The Meta Model Outline

This outline is provided as a guide to this section. Notice that there are nine linguistic distinctions in the first three categories and an additional nine in the last category. The text will also define several sub-distinctions.

I. Gathering information
      A. Referential index
      B. Nominalizations
      C. Unspecified verbs

II. Expanding limits
      A. Modal operators
      B. Universal quantifiers

III. Changing meanings
      A. Mind reading
      B. Cause and effect
      C. Lost performative
      D. Complex equivalence

IV. The Hall extensions
      A. Over/under defined terms
      B. Delusional verbal splits
      C. Either/or phrases
      D. Multiordinality
      E. Static words
      F. Pseudo words
      G. Identification
      H. Personalizing
      I. Metaphors

Note: As many of the Meta Model distinctions are described, they are linked to one or more of the communication categories described in Chapter 2. However, we need to recognize something that Hall observed: that our attempt in this work to "correlate the Meta-Model distinctions to the representational systems ... do not fit very well for most people. Undoubtedly that's why we do not find them carried over into other NLP books" (p. 142). However, we hope that this deprecation will not discourage the reader from conducting his own research to discover if and when such linguistic idiosyncrasies do combine with the other behaviors and characteristics in the communications categories model presented in Chapter 2.

Gathering Information

Referential Index

In a sentence, the person or thing doing or receiving the action of the verb is called the "referential index." In the Meta Model, these nouns are important because they are SS representations that demonstrate where the speaker has generalized, deleted, or distorted information from his DS.[8]

There are five referential index Meta Model violations. The four that follow include deleted, unspecified, generalized, and reversed referential index. The fifth distinction, nominalizations, forms its own special category.

1. *Deleted referential index* is where the speaker of the sentence simply leaves out the referent. For example, in the sentence, "The window was broken," the agent or actor of the verb "was broken" has been deleted. Of course, there are certain situations where it is obvious that more information is needed. If it were *my* window in the example above, I would immediately ask, "*Who* broke it?" However, there are many other times when lack of information in a sentence can lead to misunderstanding. The following illustration gives one example of possible consequences of deleting the referent. By the time the young woman provides the missing information, it is already too late.

Deleted referential index

When you hear a sentence in which the referent is missing, it is a cue that you need more information. Often, asking for the referent will also assist you in identifying with the speaker specific experiences that may actually be missing from his awareness. This reconnecting with the DS experience not only provides you with the missing information, it can also give the speaker an opportunity to experience a greater sense of awareness and, therefore, more choices about how to feel and behave. Hall says: "We call this questioning, meta-modeling. We ask questions that invite the person to 'go inside' to examine the very structure of the mapping and the referent experiences. This gives the other person a chance to re-map in more accurate, appropriate, and enhancing ways and to experience the new magic that arises" (p. 48). Other examples of deleted referential index with an appropriate Meta Model response are:

Speaker: I need help.
Response: What do you need help with?

Speaker: I'm being pushed into this mess.
Response: Who is pushing you?

Speaker: He's not respected.
Response: Who doesn't respect him?

In situations where a person is uncomfortable with the possibility of being confronted, but still wants to express displeasure, this violation could be used. It allows the person to say something that may be controversial or cause conflict, like "I'm being pushed into this mess" (deleting "by my boss"). Thus, the individual who might respond in an unpleasant way (his boss) has been deleted. We have observed this "safe" linguistic pattern typically being used by individuals operating from the auditory and digital representation systems.

2. *Unspecified referential index* occurs when the noun or noun phrase does not name a specific person or thing. Words like "this," "that," "it," or even "thingamabob" are all examples of unspecified referential index.

Whenever a person leaves out or does not specify important elements of a sentence, he runs the risk of being misunderstood. The following illustration demonstrates the kind of problems that can arise. In this example, the woman expresses an emotional response to something that does not necessarily relate to the man. She may, for example, be "mad" about a run in her stockings. His response to her original statement, however, indicates that he has chosen to take it personally, setting the stage for what follows. Had the woman been more specific to begin with, the whole scene would have changed dramatically.

Unspecified referential index

Other examples of this Meta Model violation are:

Speaker:	That just won't work.
Response:	What specifically won't work?

Speaker:	This is important.
Response:	What is important?

Speaker:	I don't want to talk about it.
Response:	What don't you want to talk about?

As with the previous Meta Model distinction, your goal in asking for the missing information is twofold. First, you are asking for information that will help you to better understand the speaker. This can aid in more effective communication. Second, asking for the information that is missing from the speaker's SS is one way of determining whether or not that information is even in the speaker's awareness. For example, if the speaker responded to the first question above with, "I don't know, specifically. It's just a vague sense that things aren't clicking," you immediately know several important things. You know, for example, that the individual is operating from the auditory representational system by his use of the sensory word "clicking" (see "Predicate Preference" in Chapter 2). You also know that the original stimulus for the "vague sense" is outside of his conscious awareness and, therefore, beyond his control. Discovering this about a speaker can be important in determining just what his model of the world consists of. Reconnecting a speaker with missing DS material by asking the Meta Model response questions can often provide him with a greater sense of awareness and, thus, more choices about how to feel and behave. This pattern is covered in Hall's version of the Meta Model under distinction (3) Unspecified Referential Indices (see Appendix D).

This is another Meta Model violation we have noticed being used by individuals operating from the auditory and digital representational systems. As with the previous distinction, unspecified referential index is one way to express thoughts and ideas in a way that makes them hard to challenge. By not specifying what they are talking about, "tonals" and "digitals" create a situation in which they are less likely to be contradicted.

It is important to remember that by using the appropriate responses to any of the Meta Model violations, the astute Meta Modeler gains valuable information that can increase his ability to establish rapport. He can also use the patterns to affect, often at a deep unconscious level, the speaker's model of the world. These powerful, positive linguistic interventions operate by expanding both the speaker's perception and his options for responding to the world around him.

3. *Generalized referential index* is one way the speaker can "plug the hole" left by deleting a referent. A generalized referential index is a noun or pronoun that refers to a non-specific group or category. This violation is common in the English language and is built into popular idioms like "Men don't cry" and "Women are bad drivers." In these two examples, "men" and "women" are the generalized referents. This violation is covered in Hall's version under distinction (1) Simple Deletions (see Appendix D).

As in the previous distinction, this violation often typifies people who are operating out of the tonal and digital categories. Rather than identify someone specifically who is responsible for an unpleasant situation or experience, and risk the possibility of direct confrontation, the speaker simply generalizes the referent into a non-specific category: "*People who* do those things are not very considerate" or "*One who* becomes upset at a time like this may be considered rather immature." They can even talk about themselves in this indirect manner: "If *one* were to consider such a question ..." or "There are *those who* wouldn't agree with you."

This violation can be especially important to catch when the speaker has generalized from one specific person or experience and now includes a whole category from which the original experience is only an example. In Chapter 1, for example, Sharon demonstrated as part of her model of the world the generalization: "All *men* are out to take advantage of *women*." By asking Sharon to specify who she meant by "all men" and "women," the origins of these generalizations could be determined. But, more importantly, the process of identifying non-productive and limiting portions of her model enabled Sharon to again perceive her own power in creating experience for herself. When listening for this distinction, pay attention to pronouns like "they," "everyone," "men," "women," "no one," "people," and so on and to adjectives like "all ..." and "every ...," as well as plural nouns as in "Sports *cars* are dangerous." The illustration below gives one possible outcome of such a statement, innocently spoken but poorly timed.

Generalized referential index

Other examples are:

Speaker: Loving relationships are a drain.
Response: Which loving relationship(s) do you find draining?

Speaker: Now everybody knows.
Response: Who specifically knows?

Speaker: People are so uncaring.
Response: Who, specifically, is so uncaring?

4. *Reversed referential index* occurs when the speaker is stated as receiving the action of the verb in a sentence rather than doing the action of the verb. You may recognize this pattern as being typical of someone who is depressed. Statements like "Nobody cares about me" and "I sometimes think everyone is out to get me" are examples of this pattern. In both sentences, the speaker has removed himself from a position of being "in charge" of the action and has given the power of acting to someone else. The "me," or speaker, then becomes a helpless victim of whomever or whatever is in charge. This is a pattern that appears to be common in individuals operating from the kinesthetic system.

The illustration below shows another aspect of this violation. Not only does the man apparently perceive himself as powerless, but he also fails to recognize that he is doing the very thing he is complaining about.

Reversed referential index

The famous Gestalt therapist Fritz Perls called this linguistic pattern "projection." As Martin Shepard says in *Fritz*, "whatever we believe about or see in another person or the world at large is invariably a projection. Thus a statement such as 'Nancy is a gossip' was to be rephrased as 'I am a gossip.'" He goes on to say that, as people begin to take responsibility for themselves this way, "they have the possibility of having an 'Aha!' experience, in which there is the recognition 'This is me!' This is referred to as *owning projections*" (p. 205, original emphasis).

By requiring his clients to reverse positions and become the "active" agent in the sentence, Perls would put the clients back in charge of the processes of their own existence. This transformed perception of themselves often produced some surprising insights into the model-building behaviors of his clients.

This distinction appears to play a role in Hall's expanded Meta Model distinction (8), Personalizing (see Appendix D). Also identified as a *cognitive distortion* in Rational Emotive Behavioral Therapy, Hall describes it as "The process of attaching personal significance to events and communication that could just as easily be understood impersonally" (p. 220). He goes on to observe that habitual use of this process inevitably leads to oversensitivity.

Other examples of this reversal technique are:

> Speaker: He's no good for me.
> Response: Try saying, "I'm no good for him," and tell me what you experience.

> Speaker: Everybody hates me.
> Response: Try saying this: "I hate everybody."

> Speaker: Nobody loves me.
> Response: What happens when you say "I love nobody"?

People operating out of the visual communication category often use another form of this violation. Remember that "visuals" tend to organize experiences in such a way as to prevent "contact" with those around them. One way of maintaining this distance is with the linguistic pattern of reversed referential index. The Meta Model response to these violations will be the same as those above, and you will likely get the same results, the introspective "Aha!"

Examples of this form are:

> Speaker: He never seems to understand me.
> Response: I wonder if you would mind saying, "I never seem to understand him."

> Speaker: She's the one who always seems to get us into these messes.
> Response: Try saying, "I'm the one who always get us into these messes."

Nominalizations

Linguistically, nominalization is the changing of a DS "process" into a SS "event." In other words, it is the changing of a verb that is active in time into a noun that is static or unchanging in time. Since a verb is a process word, it implies active participation by one or more elements. A noun, on the other hand, is static and unchanging. It implies no active participation by other elements. Abstract nouns called nominalizations are excellent examples of the process of distortion.

We are taught quite early in our educational experience to form abstract words. Words like "friendship," "sensation," "strategy," and so on assist us in formulating and learning creative and sophisticated concepts. But we are generally not taught to *denominalize* these words. Although the use of these words is important in our complex and technical society, they can also limit a person's sense of control over his life. It is a subtle distinction to make, but the following illustration demonstrates the power these words can have. In this case, the nominalization is the word "decision."

Nominalizations

The woman in the above illustration is talking about a "decision" in a special way. She is indicating that she no longer experiences herself in a position to change. She has given up her responsibility to get things done or to even be interested and blames it on something that she is powerless to change. This is much like the example of Sharon in Chapter 1 who talked about how her bad "relationships" kept her from getting close to anyone. As with the above illustration, when a person talks about "relationships" in this way, it can indicate a failure to recognize his active participation or responsibility in the continuing process of "relating" with another person.

The illustration below demonstrates how difficult it can be to deal with this linguistic pattern. Because she has no knowledge of the appropriate

Meta Model response, the woman in the illustration finds herself in just as helpless a position as the man who has nominalized his experience.

Nominalized individual

When a person systematically uses nominalizations like "love," "fear," or "respect," it may be a good indication that he perceives himself as having few choices and little or no control in his life. The following excerpt is from a highly "nominalized" client. Much like the young man in the illustration above, which was based on this excerpt, he is frustrated by the lack of choices he is aware of and by a strong sense that he has lost control over the events of his life.

> It's just that this darned *relationship* isn't working out. I mean, every time I turn around, it slaps me in the face. It's like I can't do anything without it being there to remind me of my *obligations*, and you know what a *pain* they can be! I tell you, I'm just tired of having all this *responsibility* shoved in my face ...

There are two easy ways to determine whether or not a word is a nominalization. One way is to say the phrase: "An ongoing ..." in your head, filling in the blank with the suspected noun. If the phrase makes sense, then it is a nominalization. Using the first italicized word in the above excerpt, the phrase "An ongoing *relationship*" makes sense. The word "relationship" is a nominalization. If we use the word "desk," as in the phrase "An ongoing *desk*," the phrase doesn't make sense. The noun "desk" is not a nominalization.

The second way to determine if a noun is a nominalization involves visualizing a wheelbarrow. It is easy to imagine placing a noun like "desk," "person," or "apple" into this imaginary wheelbarrow. These are all *concrete nouns*. Nominalizations, however, don't "fit" in our imaginary wheelbarrow. This is because they are distorted forms of verbs called abstract nouns. From the example above, they are the words "relationship," "obligations," "pain," and "responsibility."

When responding to a nominalization, it is important to assist the speaker in reconnecting with his experience so that he recognizes the role he plays in the *process* involved. By changing the noun back into a verb (what Hall – who covers this process in his model in distinction (9) Nominalizations (see Appendix D) – calls "re-languaging" it as a verb), with its actively participating elements, you assist the speaker in understanding his role as an active participant. This enables him to more easily perceive his full range of choices and the control he can exercise.

In dealing with the "nominalized" client from above, the following responses could effectively be utilized:

Speaker:	It's just that this darned relationship isn't working out.
Response:	How is the way you are relating not working out for you? (Here, the nominalization is changed back into a process word, or verb, and is used to ask for the missing information – see "Unspecified Verbs" below.)

Speaker:	I can't do anything without it being there to remind me of my obligations …
Response:	To whom are you obliged to do what?

Speaker:	You know what a pain they can be!
Response:	How do you experience that pain? (Here, in order to answer the question, the speaker must change the nominalization back into the process-verb. Again, if his answer does not give you sufficient information, simply ask for the deleted material as demonstrated in the section on unspecified verbs below.)

Speaker: I'm just tired of having responsibility shoved in my face.
Response: What do you mean "responsibility"?

Denominalizing the Medical Model

In an article entitled "Language, Emotion and Disease," Dr. Wallace Ellerbroek makes some astute, if unorthodox, observations. A staff psychiatrist at the Metropolitan State Hospital in Norwalk, California, Ellerbroek's article addresses the effects of language on our perceptions and behaviors. He contends that, "each word you use as a label for something makes you see it in an entirely different way." He cites the case of "essential" hypertension, a medical condition for which the cause is unknown. His description includes the process of denominalizing the medical term, a rare action in the field of medicine in which nominalizations abound. Contrary to the generally accepted medical model, he states:

> Remember, I called all diseases "behaviors," in other words, things that people do ... When I found a patient with elevated blood pressure (140/90 mm/Hg or more), I said to myself not "He has hypertension" but "He is hypertensioning." (1978, p. 117)

This transformation of the nominalization "hypertension," the name given to a specific set of medical conditions, back into a verb or process of "hypertensioning" not only altered Ellerbroek's perception of his patients but also his behaviors toward them. This, says Ellerbroek, changed his patients' responses to treatment in a dramatically positive way.[9]

The implication is that as we begin to alter our language, as in the above example, we change our perceptions of the *processes* of health and disease. Ultimately, this gives us more choices about our physical and emotional conditions.

A recent book captured our interest because it underscores the point above so well. David Agus, an oncologist at the University of Southern California's Westside Cancer Center and the Center for Applied Molecular Medicine, writes in *The End of Illness*:

We misunderstand cancer by making it a noun. I like to tell people that cancer isn't so much something that you "get" or "have" as it's something that the body *does*. ... Instead of saying, "Somebody has cancer," we should say, "They are cancering." We're probably cancering all the time, and our body is checking this problem in various ways to make sure that we're not cancering out of control. What keeps cancer under control is a conversation that is happening between your cells, and the language of that conversation is contained in your *proteins*." (2012, pp. 39–40)

Some individuals, especially in stressful situations, tend to dissociate from somatic sensations. It is as if they become so uncomfortable physically that they cope by removing from their conscious awareness the source of the unpleasant feelings: their bodies. Though "visuals" tend to dissociate from kinesthetic experience, it is also particularly common of "digitals." They often sound and look very removed from their bodies, their voices and movements so unanimated as to be almost robot-like. This shying away from overly expressive tonality and gestures is similar to the internal experience associated with nominalizations as opposed to the deep structure associated with verb forms. For this reason, "digitals" are said to have "nominalized" their bodies.

Digital Jobs

A person's preferred representational system may influence many aspects of his life, including his choice of careers. It may even be that the language patterns associated with the preferred system are a significant part of the job itself. The following is an example of this generalization.

If you have ever listened to two lawyers arguing a case, you may have noticed some specific linguistic patterns. One very common means of expression is the deletion of themselves (deleted referential index) from the conversations and replacing the "spaces" with nominalizations. Such phrases as "statistics demonstrate" and "studies have shown," as well as "the situation calls for" and "under the present circumstances," are combined with an incredible array of legal jargon. This is quite common coming from a person whose preferred representational system is the digital system.

Unspecified Verbs

All verbs are unspecified in that they only symbolize an experience or process; they are not that experience or process. However, for our purposes, there are degrees of specificity within the group of words we call verbs. For example, to say that someone "touched" me is much more generalized than to say that someone "caressed" me. Both verbs imply contact with my person; however, the verb "caressed" is more specific about the kind of contact involved. Another example of the use of unspecified verbs is given in the following scene:

> As I walked up to the young lady on the bench, she wiped a tear from her eye and asked, "Why does my husband always hurt me?"

This is a good example of an often-used unspecified verb, "hurt." Again we are faced with the choice of "going inside" and creating the missing information or we can simply ask for it. The potential for creating a misrepresentation of the situation is much less likely when we ask for the information. If we try to "make up" the missing material, we might decide, for example, that the young lady was beaten by her husband. Or we might guess that he has been mean to her and she is talking about an emotional "hurt." Either way, we won't know for sure without asking.

Hall talks about two very different linguistic patterns: one is sensory-based, what he describes as see-hear-feel descriptions, and the other is evaluative-based and describes attributions of value or meaning and leads to "mental constructs" such as concepts, abstractions, and relationships. Unspecified verbs fall into the latter pattern. As Hall says, "Can you track those words to your mental screen? No you can't. Whatever you fill in about [a word like love], you invented it. It came from your model of the world, not from the language itself" (pp. 48–49). The point is that in order to avoid the mistake of assuming you understand a speaker who uses an unspecified verb you can ask for the missing part of the speaker's model of the world.

This Meta Model violation plays a part in a number of Hall's distinctions as follows: (3) Unspecified Referential Indices (Unspecified Nouns and Verbs), (4) Unspecified Processes (Adverbs Modifying Verbs), and (5) Unspecified Processes (Adjectives Modifying Nouns) (see Appendix D).

The following illustration provides an example of the potential unpleasant effects of such non-specific communication patterns. In this case, the unspecified verb is "show."

Unspecified verbs

Other examples of this violation and appropriate responses are:

Speaker: I feel bad.
Response: What are you feeling bad about?

Speaker: She is really hard on me.
Response: How is she hard on you?

Speaker: He could demonstrate some concern.
Response: How would you like him to demonstrate concern?

Sometimes the speaker's response to your request for more information will indicate rules within his model of the world (see "Individual Constraints" in Chapter 1). In the last example above, the speaker might respond to the question, "How would you like him to demonstrate concern?" with "He could answer more quickly." This rule, demonstrating concern = answering quickly, could have special importance in understanding the communication process of this person in certain situations. This type of rule is discussed in detail in the Meta Model distinction complex equivalence below.

This Meta Model violation, unspecified verbs, is particularly common to individuals operating out of the kinesthetic category. *They* know what they mean by predicates like "hurt," "feels good/bad," "deeply moved," "entangled," and so on, and they tend to assume that everyone else knows what they mean. Since this can lead to confusion and misunderstanding, it is often important to challenge this violation.

Since this is a special case of deletion, again your goal is to obtain the information necessary for a complete understanding of the statement as well as discover more about the speaker's model of the world. As you continue to do this, you will begin to discover consistencies in the speaker's model. Attending to these consistencies will assist you in becoming a more effective communicator and will facilitate the entire process of change.

Expanding Limits

The next two distinctions are valuable as a means of assisting in the process of expanding the speaker's model of the world. By gaining more choices about how to feel and think and what to be aware of, the speaker gains more control over how to act and respond in situations that are uncomfortable or painful.

Meta Model Diagram #2

The remaining Meta Model responses involve challenging directly or indirectly limits that are discovered in the speaker's model of the world. These limits are initially presented in the form of the speaker's SS. By using the appropriate Meta Model responses, the boundaries of the DS are defined.

Challenging the boundaries expands the speaker's model. The expansion first takes place with the SS and then generalizes to the speaker's model of the world

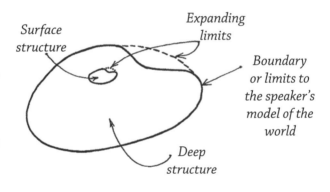

Challenging these limits linguistically can assist the speaker in breaking through confining model limits or restrictions. The results are more choices about how to feel, see, and hear the world as well as alternatives to behavior that have been unsatisfactory, painful, or limiting.

Modal Operators

Modal operator is a linguistic term meaning "mode of operation." These expressions define certain boundaries of the person's model of the world.

To extend beyond these boundaries may invite some *catastrophic expectation* over which the speaker believes he has no control. Bringing this expectation into the conscious awareness of the speaker enables him to test and evaluate its validity. If the limit is found to be unreasonable, the boundaries can be removed from that portion of the speaker's model of the world. This process gives the speaker more choices about his thoughts and feelings. It expands his awareness and allows him to develop alternative behaviors in response to similar situations. The two types of modal operators are described below.

Note: Hall describes both in his distinction (7) Modal Operators (Operational Modes of Being), and he also adds modal operators of desire (want) and of choice (will) in his model (see Appendix D).

1. *Modal operators of necessity* are exemplified by the imperative "should."[10] For example, someone might say, "I really should be more flexible at times like this." The appropriate Meta Model response is, "What do you think would happen if you weren't more flexible?" This form of question requires that the speaker bring into awareness the underlying potentially catastrophic expectation that elicited the original statement. If upon examination he determines that it is valid, that the limit is appropriate and functional, then he can choose to retain it as useful. If, however, it turns out to be a limit that is causing him undue pain or is preventing more appropriate behavior or growth, then it can be explored for its functional elements or discarded in the light of new choices. The illustration below shows both the modal operator of necessity and the "catastrophic" expectation. The two are often not presented together, and sometimes the speaker is surprised to discover just what his expectation is.

Modal operator of necessity

Other words that imply a lack of choice or indicate the speaker's lack of awareness of his participation in and responsibility for his feelings and actions are "must," "have to," "ought to," and their opposites, "shouldn't," "must not," and so on. Examples of this Meta Model violation are:

Speaker: I must never say those things.
Response: What will happen if you do?

Speaker: I ought to be understanding when he's like that.
Response 1: What do you imagine would happen if you weren't?
Response 2: (Shift to another modal operator) Try saying, "I *can be* understanding when he's like that." Now describe your experience.

Speaker: I have to believe in it.
Response 1: What do you think would happen if you didn't believe in it?
Response 2: Say it this way: "I choose to believe in it," and tell me how that feels.

"Shoulds" are often heard when one person is blaming another: "You should know better than that!" This pattern is typical of someone operating out of the visual communication category, especially under stress. In this way, a "visual" can verbally externalize his frustration or anger at a person or situation and at the same time exclude himself from having any responsibility for the situation.

2. A *modal operator of possibility* is another linguistic marker of a potentially counterproductive limitation on a person's model of the world. When a person says, "I can't," he is talking about something he perceives as being outside his ability or sphere of influence. However, it is often simply the person's perception that is limiting, not his ability or the environment or the situation. In the illustration below, for example, the first boy's initial statement followed by his catastrophic expectation is a demonstration of a limit on his model of the world that prevents him from even attempting to get what he wants.

Modal operator of possibility

Being presented with a modal operator of possibility can be an excellent opportunity for you to explore with the speaker a limitation or boundary to his model of the world. By responding with the questions, "What stops you?" or "What would happen if you did?" you begin to assist the speaker in determining the validity of the limit and how functional or dysfunctional it is for him. Again, this question brings into awareness the usually unconscious catastrophic expectation in such a way that it can be dealt with. Other examples from this linguistic pattern are:

Speaker: I couldn't say something like that.
Response: What would stop you? What would happen if you did?

Speaker: I can't do that.
Response 1: What do you imagine would happen if you did do it? What would you need in order to be able to do it?
Response 2: Humor me: Try saying, "I can do that," and tell me what you experience differently.

Speaker: It is not possible for me to love anymore.
Response 1: What stops you from loving?
Response 2: What might happen if you did?

When people who are operating out of the kinesthetic category are under stress, they tend to perceive themselves as having no control, of being "at the mercy" of the situation or of the individuals involved. In this case, it is common for them to use the linguistic form, "I can't ...," because it fits their internal representation of the situation.

The Challenge

Remember, when you begin to challenge a person's model of the world, you may at times shake the very foundations of his belief systems. It is exciting when people begin to understand that they *do* have control in situations where they thought they didn't, and they *can* actually change their thoughts, feelings, and behaviors. However, the sudden realization of this additional responsibility may also be uncomfortable or even traumatic to some. Be prepared to provide additional support and understanding to people who begin to make dramatic changes in themselves and their models of reality.

Universal Quantifiers

Universal quantifiers are words that imply or state absolute conditions about the speaker's perception of reality. In his model in distinction (6) Universal Quantifiers, Hall calls these "allness words" (see Appendix D). They often indicate that a generalization has been made from a specific experience in the speaker's life. In Chapter 1, the case study client Sharon expressed during a session that she believed "all men are out to take advantage of women." She had generalized from several unpleasant experiences with *some* men to a generalization that *all* men behaved in a particular way. Linguistically, her use of the word "all," a universal quantifier, indicated that such a generalization had been made. As it was in her case, it can be important to challenge this generalization. This enables a person to discover if his model is limiting his experience of the world in ways that may be causing undue pain. In the illustration below, the man is so wrapped up in his particular frame of mind that he runs the risk of failing to perceive the happy welcome by his beautiful, healthy family. This is typical of the way universal quantifiers can be indicative of a distorted model of the world.

Universal quantifiers

By helping a speaker to recognize that such statements are generalizations that are not necessarily based on reality, you begin the process of expanding and changing perceptions that limit and cause the person to suffer needlessly. The Meta Model response to phrases that include words like "always," "never," "all," "nothing ever," and so on is to ask the speaker if he is aware of any contradictions to his statement. Another effective response is to repeat his statement while exaggerating with your voice the universal quantifiers in order to demonstrate the absurdity or impossibility of the statement. Some examples are:

Speaker: I never do anything right.
Response: Can you think of a time when you did something right?

Speaker: Everybody's mean to me.
Response: *Everybody's always* mean to you, *everyone* you know, even your best friend, even the milk man?

Speaker: Nothing special ever happens to me.
Response: I wonder if you can remember at least one time when something special did happen to you.

On the Lighter Side

Humor can have an important place in the therapeutic setting. When the client comes in and is under a great deal of stress and pain, the seriousness of the situation may at times pervade the session. However, humor is an important part of our experience, and when we can laugh at ourselves, it is sometimes easier to accept and change our foibles and failings. The therapist who can utilize humor to lighten, without making light of, the process of change and discovery can often use this talent to quickly gain and maintain positive rapport with his client.

One interesting and useful aspect of universal quantifiers is that they often have built-in, potentially therapeutic *double binds*.[11] These can be used to assist the speaker in rapidly expanding the implied limit as in the following examples:

Upon hearing the client say, "Though I want to, I'll *never* respect her; I *always* get what I want from her," the therapist responded with: "I have a homework assignment for you. During the coming week I would like for you to ask her to give you only what you want in order to respect her."

When one client entered, saying, "You know, I've *never* learned anything from a therapy session," the counselor responded with: "Well, then, your task for today is to learn one thing for certain, and that is that you can learn nothing from this session."

Changing Meanings

This final section of the Meta Model concerns the logical meanings (semantics) of the words in a person's SS. The following Meta Model violations all have in common the characteristics of either incompleteness or logical impossibility. The words and phrases in this category make up some of the most challenging and useful points from which to embark on the journey into exploring and expanding the speaker's model of the world.

Mind Reading

This is the concept that a person can know what other people are feeling or thinking – what their internal experiences are – without verifying it with them.

Mind reading

This surreptitious presupposition of another's internal state can be the cause of much pain and misunderstanding. As in the above illustration, mind reading can prevent a person from achieving personal goals.[12] This is a case where the phrase, "If only she *really* knew how he feels ..." really makes sense!

When someone makes a statement that implies knowledge of another's internal emotional state or thoughts, there are two Meta Model responses you can make. One response can be made only if the person about whom the statement has been made is available. Simply ask the mind reader to check out his statement with that person. If his perception is inaccurate, the other person can assist the speaker in more precisely tuning in to his true thoughts or feelings. Consistently asking individuals in therapy and in other settings to check out their mind-reading statements with the people involved sets a good example for more accurate involvement in the process of relating with others.

The other Meta Model response is to simply ask the speaker, "How do you know?" Often his response will give you a surprising amount of information about how he perceives the world around him. You may also get indications of personal rules (see Chapter 2) that the speaker utilized in building and maintaining his model of reality. In the above illustration, if the woman were asked how she "knew" that the man "isn't even interested," her response might be: "Well, he never seems to look me straight in the eye when we talk. And he doesn't seem to notice when I wear something nice." With this information you now know that, for her, looking her straight in the eye and commenting on her clothes means that you are "interested." This can be particularly important information to have in a family setting or in other close relationships. The following excerpt from a family therapy session exemplifies how this linguistic pattern often occurs.

> Jack, having arrived late to the session, immediately turned to his wife, saying, "I know what you're thinking, all of you! You're disappointed in me. You think I've failed you again. You don't even like me anymore. I'm just a 'bum' to you. Oh, I know you won't admit it, but I can tell."

Somehow, Jack has decided that he already knows what is in each person's head, what their thoughts and feelings are. Having arrived late to the session, these ideas of his are not based on any "concrete" evidence. This is coming from his own expectations, from his own model of the world. This is easily demonstrated by the responses of the other family members to his verbal "outbreak" as he walked into the room. His wife, Joan, speaks first, then their 17-year-old daughter Susan:

Joan (speaking softly):	Where did that come from? You know, Jack, I was just about to tell you how happy I was to see you. I want you to know I'm glad you decided to come (Joan starts to cry), and I don't think you're a bum ... I love you.
Susan:	Me too, daddy. What makes you think we're disappointed in you? I'm just glad you're here.

The therapist next asked, "Jack, what was it that led you to think that everyone was disappointed in you, that they didn't like you and thought you were a bum?" Jack's response tells us a great deal about his model of the world, including some of his own personal rules.

Well, I don't know. When I walked in, I saw that everyone was sitting with their arms folded, you know, like they were all mad or something. When I went to sit down by my wife, she wouldn't look at me, she just kept staring at the floor, you know, like people do when they're pissed off. I know that look! Susie, there, she just frowned at me, like I was some kind of bum, you know, some stranger. I've done a lot of things I shouldn't have; it would serve me right if nobody liked me!

Calibrated Communication

Mind reading plays a special part in *calibrated communication* or *calibrated loops*. These are unconscious, often pain-producing patterns of communication that can be observed between individuals in couples and in families.[13] Bostic St. Clair and Grinder observe:

> We "know" that our spouse or close friend is not in a mood to consider positively an offer to dine or go to the theatre by the tone of voice, or posture, or breathing pattern or more likely, by the Gestalt or overall physiological pattern he or she presents to us unconsciously and which we typically detect and respond to unconsciously. If, in fact, we have calibrated accurately and are not presently hallucinating (projecting) our own emotions, such calibrations serve as the basis for successfully reading the people around us. (2001, p. 165)

However, Hall cautions against mistaking *intimate calibration* with "mind reading." This is where individuals living together "become highly calibrated to the other's style, states, and orientation" (p. 113) and eventually begin to believe they can actually read the mind of the other.

The excerpt from the session with Jack and his family revealed that Joan's staring at the floor meant something specific to Jack. His "I know that look" indicated at least a partial awareness on his part of a familiar pattern of communication between them. This "loop," the sequence of "the look" and his response to it, was repeated several times during the session. Whenever Jack's wife stared at the floor, he became sullen and uncomfortable. His response was not related to the content of the ongoing conversation but was based on minor *subliminal cues*. These are unconscious non-verbal communications that have special meanings to the individuals involved. These special meanings are often an important part of an individual's complex equivalence (see below). In Jack's case, looking at the floor = being pissed off. As a therapist, counselor, or any person who works with people, your ability to recognize and bring these patterns into the awareness of those involved can help disarm their harmful effects.

Mind reading is insidious in that it can work in two ways. One way, demonstrated in the previous examples, comes out as "I know what you're thinking." The other form of mind reading occurs when a person believes that others should know what *he* is thinking or feeling. The illustration below is an example of this form of reversed or *projected mind reading*.

Projected mind reading

When this pattern is used, the speaker reverses the mind reading and projects it onto others. The woman in the illustration, for example, believes that since she "knows" without asking what makes the man happy, then he "should know" without asking what makes her happy. Challenging this form of mind reading is just as important as challenging the other form. Some examples of the mind-reading distinctions are:

Speaker: I know what is good for him.
Response: How do you know what is good for him?

Speaker: I can tell she doesn't like me.
Response: How can you tell she doesn't like you?

Speaker: He should know better.
Response: How should he know not to do that?

Speaker: If she really cared about me, she wouldn't have to ask what I need.

Response: If she doesn't ask, then how will she know for sure what you need?

The mind-reading pattern is often associated with people operating out of the visual communication category. It can come out in an accusing "I know what you're thinking!" or in the more direct "You ought to know better than that!" This linguistic form implies a need in the speaker to be in control of the environment through omniscient "knowing" and is often communicated with the "I shouldn't have to tell you" format.

Cause and Effect

Cause and effect is a particularly widespread and potentially pain-producing Meta Model violation. It is the belief that an action such as a verbal or facial expression can *cause* another person to experience a definite emotion or "inner state." The person responding believes he has no choice in how to respond. A statement like "You make me mad" implies that there is no other possible way to respond. It is as if the speaker has relinquished all responsibility for creating his own emotional state. The fallacy of the cause and effect presuppositions becomes apparent when some action by one person results in completely different responses from others involved, as in the illustration below.

Cause and effect: different responses

There are two ways in which cause and effect belief systems can bring about pain or unhappiness. First, the belief that someone else can create in you an emotional state implies that you have no control over your own feelings or thoughts. Without this control, not only are you unable to change your inner experience in order to become more comfortable, but you are also dependent on others to create "good" feelings inside of you.

Second, since you believe that you can cause another person to experience pleasurable emotions, then you can also cause them to experience pain and sorrow. With this "power" comes a sense of responsibility as the "causal agent." When you "make" someone sad, then you feel guilty and often want to know if there is "anything I can do" to "make them feel better." Within this belief system, it is possible to persecute yourself for something that you actually have no control over, since you cannot cause or create a different outcome. The effects of this pattern are illustrated below. The man finds himself in a quandary as a result of his cause and effect belief system. Questioning these quasi-causal connections can often assist a person in experiencing more choices and much less pain and guilt in his life.

Cause and effect

During a seminar on the Meta Model we were once questioned by a young woman who firmly believed that the feelings and emotions of a client are very much in the hands of the therapist. She stated her belief that a therapist has a "duty and responsibility to ensure that a client doesn't 'feel bad.'" Though we agreed that "irresponsible behavior" on the part of any people helper is unethical, we maintained the premise that one person cannot take responsibility as the *causal agent* for another's emotions. The following transcript from that seminar gives one possible response to this cause and effect belief system.

L/P:	Then you're saying that it isn't right to go around "pushing other people's buttons"?
Woman:	Not if it might make them feel bad. You have an obligation, especially with clients, to say things in a way that will make them feel better.
L/P:	You mean, then, that it is important to push the "good-feelings" buttons?
Woman:	Yes, exactly. As a therapist you're in a position to selectively push the buttons that will make the client feel better.
L/P:	What you're saying then, is that, if you were my client, it would be possible for me to push your buttons. Please tell me quickly, are they on the front of you or on your back? I wouldn't want to push a wrong one by accident!

After the laughter died down – the woman laughed good-naturedly too – we continued, saying, "Seriously, we think it's important for each of you to decide for yourself just where those 'buttons' are and whether you believe they are on the inside or on the outside. If they're on the outside, seek professional help immediately! If they're on the inside, well, then, thank goodness. At least you know who pushes them now, don't you!"

By challenging this belief system when it is being counterproductive or causing undue pain, you can assist the speaker in having more choices about how to feel and operate in the world. There are two ways to challenge this violation. Ask the speaker to tell you how, specifically, he caused the other person to feel that way. Or ask how the other person makes the speaker feel a particular way. This will give you a great deal of information about how the speaker makes sense of the world and how he perceives himself in relation to others. This information may be invaluable in the ongoing processes of positive change and growth. Hall covers this distinction in his model at (11) Cause–Effect (see Appendix D).

This pattern is typical of the person acting from the kinesthetic communication category. Generally, it comes out as "You hurt me when you say those things" (I have no control over my feelings) or "I'm sorry if I've hurt your feelings" (I don't deserve this power over you; I feel guilty for using it). Some examples and Meta Model responses are:

Speaker: Their laughter makes me mad.
Response: How does their laughing cause you to be mad?

Speaker: She upsets me.
Response: What, specifically, does she do that you feel upset about?

Speaker: I feel bad for making her cry.
Response: What did you do that you believe made her cry?

Choices

It is not always necessary to challenge directly the cause and effect belief system in the therapeutic setting. When people present this pattern in their SS, it is sometimes more important to bring into their conscious awareness the specific behaviors that they believe to be the cause of the emotional states. By maintaining a *meta-perspective* – an awareness of the *pattern* involved – you can effectively lead the speaker to an understanding of the concept in ways that are more relevant to them personally. In this way you would not deal directly with the more abstract ideology that underlies their belief system but would concentrate on more pragmatic, practical implications of the pattern.

One mistaken notion sometimes arises during the teaching of the concept of cause and effect to groups. Some people think it implies that a person may do whatever he likes regardless of others. We would like to stress that a person who is behaving in a responsible manner is cognizant enough of others to take into account how they *may choose* to respond to his behaviors. Most individuals do not care to spend time with someone who behaves in a way that is unpleasant to them. People learn early what kinds of behavior will get them what they want, and these are incorporated into their models of the world. Everyone is always acting in accordance with these models.

Lost Performative

Lost performative refers to judgments, beliefs, or standards expressed by a person in such a way that the individual who is making the judgment or setting the standard is not identified in the speaker's SS. These statements usually come out as generalizations about the world, and they have no apparent connection with the speaker. In the illustration below, it is hard to tell whether the girl is simply "parroting" something she has heard or actually believes what she is saying. Of course, the boy's response to her initial statement indicates what he thinks about the matter!

Lost performative

Only too often these generalized statements about the world come from the speaker's own model. By linguistically leaving himself out as the evaluator or judge, the speaker indicates the possibility that there are limits within his model that he doesn't recognize as being self-imposed. By requesting the speaker to identify the "judge" who is making these value judgments, you can assist him in confronting those limits or rules in his model of the world. Once they have been identified, they can be challenged for their validity, especially if they are preventing the speaker from experiencing a fuller, richer life.

Some examples of this violation that are often indicative of unconscious, limiting rules are:

Speaker: That's a stupid thing to do.
Response: That's stupid according to whom?

Speaker: Oh, it's not important anyway.
Response: It's not important to whom?

Speaker: It's not good to be strict.
Response: Not good to whom?

By getting the speaker to use such phrases as "*I think* ..." or "*My* belief is ..." the speaker is able to identify himself as the specific performer of the judgment, thought, belief, or action. Without that identification, any challenge to the belief system is irrelevant.

Hall covers this Meta Model violation in his model at distinction (8) Lost Performative (see Appendix D). However, he also presents a similar pattern at (2) Comparative and Superlative Deletions (or Unspecified Relations) in which the speaker uses adjectives that end in *-er* and *-est* but fails to identify the referent being compared to or the basis for the comparison, as in the following examples:

Speaker: I feel closer to her.
Response: Closer than whom?

Speaker: He's better for you.
Response: Better than whom? Better according to what standard?

Speaker: I think he's the smartest.
Response: Smartest based on what measure? Smartest compared to whom?

In keeping with their tendency to be "nominalized" – removing themselves from any position that might leave them open to criticism or challenge – "tonals" and "digitals" both commonly use this pattern. It is possible to make sweeping generalizations, profound truths, and important judgments and not ever identify yourself as the originator of such. An example of this pattern is: "Statistically speaking, results demonstrate that under prime conditions it is considered in the *best* interests of all concerned that it is *important* to be assertive."

Complex Equivalence

We touched on this pattern in Chapter 1. As described by Bandler and Grinder, "The client says two Surface Structures which are separated by a pause and have the same syntactic form" (1975, p. 89). Hall describes this complex generalization as a pattern that often links two phenomena that are at different logical levels. For example, you hear a man say, "I know my wife doesn't agree with me. She won't look at me." The second statement is a verifiable event. It can be described in sensory terms (what Hall calls a "see-hear-feel referent"). However, it is linked to the first statement of *knowing* about the internal state of another person (*agreeing*) as if it were also verifiable by the senses. But this statement is at a different logical level. You may notice that this statement is also an example of mind reading.

There are two Meta Model responses that can be used to recover the generalized and deleted information in such a case and invite the speaker to explore possible limitations of his map of the territory as represented by the statements.

The first is to *verify the equivalence* by asking for confirmation: "So her not looking at you means that she disagrees with you?" If the individual does not agree with the statement, you can ask for the missing information: "Well then, how do you know she disagrees with you?" and continue to meta-model the responses.

However, if the person confirms this belief, then *shift the referential index* by asking, "When *you* don't look at *her*, does that mean you disagree with her?" If the person accepts this new complex generalization, it would be easiest to move to the second Meta Model response below. Generally, however, the individual will not accept this new generalization: "No, that's different." At this point, you can begin to explore how the two situations are different. This will ultimately lead to a discussion about how to verify the internal state of his wife to ensure he accurately understands her behavior.

The second Meta Model response is to *exaggerate the pattern* with a universal quantifier: "Does it *always* mean she disagrees with you when she doesn't look at you? *Every* time?" This challenges the generalization. If the speaker responds with, "Well, not *every* time," he invites a discussion about how he might verify his assumption or belief by asking her to describe what she is actually experiencing.

In our example in the illustration on page 32, rather than a verbal pattern as described by Bandler and Grinder above, the "boss" in the illustration *internalized* the woman's verbal request for "more respect" as *meaning* she wanted a new office. He then failed to verify his complex equivalence by asking for a more complete representation (a see-hear-feel referent) of what she meant by *respect*. Had he done so, had he challenged his own mind-reading pattern, he might have put the cost of refurbishing the office towards the pay raise she really wanted. By the same token, when we use words such as respect, trust, love, and so on, we can forestall such misunderstandings by defining the meaning in more concrete or sensory terms. For example, if the employee had said: "I deserve more respect on this job," and then added, "One way you could show it would be to give me a raise," she might have had a more satisfactory outcome!

The Hall Extensions to the Meta Model

It is easier for trained specialists to change their terminology than to re-educate semantically the rest of the race.

Alfred Korzybski, *Science and Sanity*

What follows are the nine distinctions identified by Hall that extend the Meta Model originally developed by Bandler and Grinder. Part of the magic of Hall's presentation is his emphasis on the neuro-linguistics and neuro-semantics of the Meta Model and his descriptions of just how language is incorporated into everything we *do* and everything we *are*. His exceptional insight into the fabric of language in our lives is revealed in the following:

> Even though our representations at any level may not accord with, or fit, the territory at all (and may even represent *nothing at all* in the territory!), *as* we represent *and* then develop other thoughts-and-feelings (beliefs) *about* those representations, so we construct a system of thoughts-and-feelings about those. These higher level cause–effect relationships, complex equivalences, presuppositions, etc. will indeed become *actualized* (literally, real-ized) in the body. The representations will become somatized and then govern our neurology. It is in this way that our *mind* becomes *muscle*, that ideas and concepts become *embodied* in us. (2001, p.153, original emphasis)

Over/Under Defined Terms

According to Hall, Korzybski (1994) noted that certain words and phrases are simultaneously over- and under-defined. This Meta Model distinction comes into play when we use terms that overgeneralize and confuse our "verbal maps" with the territory (known linguistically as *intension*) while at the same time systematically under-define by failing to link the terms to more concrete referents (known linguistically as *extension*). Such words and phrases are over-defined by intension (they depend more on internally generated experience such as social and individual constraints covered in Chapter 1) and under-defined by extension (not providing enough empirical details to define their meaning). In an e-mail exchange with Hall while preparing this section, he wrote:

> In other words, the term does not have enough extension of it through indexing what, when, where, with whom, how, in what way, etc. So "husband" or "wife" does not have enough specific and precise details about John or Mary. But "husband" or "wife" is over-defined by intension --- that is, by abstract ideas and conceptual understandings of what a "husband" or "wife" should be [or] ought to be. So the person marries a good "husband" or a good "wife" and then is surprised about the extensional facts that come along with John or Mary.

Many evaluative words lack obvious external referents while implying rich internal contexts such as "good," "bad," "ugly," "useful," and "counter-productive". In addition, words like "assistant," "teacher," "husband," and "wife" also lack sensory-based definitions and depend on a person's own experiences (internally generated memories, perceptions, social expectations, and so on) to define the term. We don't know from the expression "He's my assistant," for example, the more complete extensional definition that would answer questions about what exactly *that* assistant does, when they do it and with whom, where, how, and so on. If a speaker uses the phrase "an effective solution," for example, without more information (like a more complete "verbal diagram" or as in the example below a *visual* diagram) it is impossible to fully understand what the speaker means.

Over/under defined terms

On the positive side, this process of using internally defined terms is essential to our ability to fantasize, but if we don't regularly perform reality checks on our assumptions we run the risk of failing to adjust ourselves to the "real" world. When you hear someone using expressions that imply "reality" but that actually require you to "hallucinate" the meaning from your own model of the world, ask the speaker to more fully define (*extensionalize*) them:

Speaker:	He's just spoiled rotten.
Response:	What do you mean by "spoiled"? What does he do or say that leads you to make that judgment about him?

Speaker:	She's such a mean person!
Response:	Mean how and in what context? Mean based on what or according to whose standard?

Speaker:	That won't be a very effective solution.
Response:	What, why, when, where, how is it trying to resolve? Not effective based on what results? What will prevent it from being effective?

Delusional Verbal Splits

Our ability to alter the world linguistically and conceptually enables us to efficiently categorize our experiences in order to plan, create, and so on. However, breaking certain phenomena into parts that do not actually exist can also prevent us from attaining goals or from overcoming ineffective patterns of thinking behavior. Delusional verbal splits occur as a result of the linguistic or conceptual "splintering" of reality into distinct aspects (known as *elementalism*). This can be particularly problematic when we apply this compartmentalizing to processes such as communicating and relating. Imagine how the concepts behind the speakers' statements in the following examples, if left unchallenged, would have the "power" to block perception of potential alternate realities.

Speaker:	My spontaneous soul resists my tendency to want to plan ahead.
Response:	If you were to merge your "spontaneous soul" with your "organized self," what would you be like? (*integrating* the parts) What have you done in the past that satisfies all of you?

Speaker:	That's the part of her I don't much like.
Response:	What is the behavior she exhibits that you don't like? How is that different from when she is behaving in ways you do like? Remember, she is the same woman, regardless of how she is behaving!

Either/Or Phrases

We live in an extremely complex world. There are times when it is appropriate, even necessary, to limit our choices by narrowing our perception of choice down. This process of simplification, however, can also work against us. Oversimplified either/or statements indicate a map of the world that allows for only two options for how to view, value, or respond to aspects and events of our lives. With this mindset, there is no middle ground or gray areas, no ambiguity, no "both-and" perceptions. The goal in meta-modeling this pattern is to assist the speaker to recognize other options, as in the illustration.

The intervention by the male teacher in the above example opens the door to additional information that might prove invaluable for working with the young student. Additional examples include:

Speaker:	If I don't graduate, I'll never find a good job.
Response:	(Do a *reality-check* with the speaker) Do you know anyone who didn't graduate who had a good job? Steve Jobs didn't graduate, but as CEO of Apple he had a pretty good job! What is there between CEO of Apple and where you are now that you would be happy with that doesn't require a degree?

Speaker:	Either he is stupid or he doesn't know how to pay attention.
Response:	(Ask for a *wider frame*) What if he is neither? What if there is something else is going on?

Either/or phrases

Speaker: They're either too tired or too bored to continue.

Response: So, you believe they are either too tired or too bored. What was happening just before you came to this conclusion that might have affected their motivation to continue?

Multiordinality

Multiordinality refers to the fact that many words can be used at different levels of abstraction. Each different use of the word might be considered a distinct ordinal (numbered) level, and as Hall points out, "What's deleted in multiordinal terms is the *level* or dimension of abstraction" (p. 197, original emphasis), making the meaning of the word in and of itself ambiguous. Korzybski (1994) points out that these terms allow "great versatility in expression, as our most important vocabulary consists of *m.o.*terms, which can be extended indefinitely by assigning many different orders and, therefore, meanings." (p. 436, original emphasis)

Take the process of *thinking* and change it into the noun *thoughts* for example, and you create the first level of this abstraction. Using this form of the word, it is now acceptable to *own your own thoughts*. At the second level of abstraction, you can have *thoughts* about your *thoughts* or *second thoughts*. The word is the same, but the meaning has shifted.

Words such as "love," "satisfaction," "insanity," and "ethics," by their nature, conjure up a multitude of meanings and invite us to invent our own meanings, because they are so ambiguous. Hall uses the word "love" to demonstrate the different levels. In the first level love is defined by certain feelings and thoughts about specific people or things: "I love Pam" or "I love pizza" for example. Bump it up a level and you have "I love being in love with Pam" which might be called infatuation. Then, if you say that you love the fact that you love loving Pam, at this third level you would be called a romantic. The word stays the same, but the meaning changes depending on the level at which it is used.

In order to be sure you correctly understand multiordinal terms, you need to ask for the speaker's definition. This will include variables such as when, where or how the term is used or the *context* in which it is used. As Korzybski (1994) notes, "in a context its meaning is single and fixed by that context." When encountering such words or phrases, there are several options with the speaker to explore the missing information:

Speaker: I hate work. (Because this could mean the speaker hates the *act* of working but just as well could mean he hates his *job*; there is ambiguity in his statement.)

Response 1:   (*Contextualize the referents* by asking for the ambiguous referent or for time and/or place referents) What kind of work don't you like? Is it school work, housework, dental work, work on the job, and so on? When/where are you most likely to feel that way about work?

Response 2:   (You can also *chunk down* by asking for specificity) What about working don't you like? What are you most likely to be doing when you feel that way about work? Where are you usually when you start feeling that way about work?

Static Words

Also known as *signal words*, static words occur when we take a vague or ambiguous multiordinal term (see above) and lock it into a fixed and rigid context resulting in a single meaning, and then operate as if there is no other possible meaning for the word or phrase. Because the context implies that it is absolute and "true for all time," it is easy to forget that it is just a construct, making it likely we will eventually assume it accurately represents reality. Such "pronouncements from heaven" indicate a dogmatic way of thinking that finds the speaker "stuck in a quagmire" of his own making. We call this process of giving in to the belief that the descriptor is reality as *losing quotes*, because it is as if we forget that they are only words. The illustration shows what can happen when someone loses quotes regarding a particularly limiting static word. "This is insanity!" "Love conquers all," and "Life sucks" are examples of this mode of thinking.

Static words

The unfortunate individual in the illustration above has become "stuck" by his own very pessimistic definition of life. The challenge to static words is to help the speaker reconnect such "pronouncements" with their referent processes in reality and is a process itself:

Speaker: Life sucks.

Response 1:   (As with multiordinal terms, ask the speaker to *contextualize* the word) Whose life are you talking about? What about it sucks?

Response 2:   (*Re-vitalize* the word by adding back the hidden processes and verbs) How are you living such that you feel life "sucks"? What is going on that makes you feel this way?

Response 3:   (*De-infinitize* the state by helping the speaker to identify stages or variables) Does it suck all the time or only at certain times? Did it always suck, or did something happen to make you feel that way?

Response 4:   (Help the speaker reconnect with a more realistic understanding that the word is not an accurate reflection of reality) What do you mean by "life"? How does your frame of
mind when you believe "life sucks" compare or contrast to
those times when you are happy or content with life?

Pseudo Words

Hall calls pseudo words "verbal fictions." These *fake* or *false* word symbols
are nominalized process words that are completely disconnected from any
referents. They are *maps* that represent absolutely *no* associated *territory*.
The word "heat" when used as a verb (*to heat*) describes a process; however, when used as a noun, it is a fiction, because there is no actual *thing*
that can be named heat.

Certain words in this category that perpetrate a fictitious model of the
world are often used to amplify emotional perceptions of events and situations, such as "tragic," "terrible," "horrible," "awful," and so on. When we
hear such expressions, we are tempted to suspend caution and can easily be deluded and deceived into accepting the *non-real* territory of the
speaker. As Hall says, "If we language unsanely, using words without true
referents, we will begin to think-feel unsane and respond to the ghosts of
our words" (p. 209). As the illustration below shows, one person's perceptions of events may be significantly different from another's. The more
pseudo words are "rehearsed" (either externally or internally as self-talk
or internal dialog), the more the person will believe them to be factual,
even in light of contrary evidence as the illustration below demonstrates.

Pseudo words

Challenging these non-words can be as important to our own equilibrium as to the health of our clients. You can help a speaker who is using such words to overcome their delusions and open to new, less emotional and more productive generalizations by asking them to define their pseudo words.

This is one of those areas where the question "Why?" is extremely useful:[14]

Speaker: I had a *terrible* time! It was really *awful*!
Response: Why was it terrible? Explain what you mean by "terrible."
                What made it so awful?

Speaker: I just can't get over the *horrible* insults he made.
Response 1:   What about his insults were "horrible"? Can you be more
                specific: what did he actually say that you believe was "filled
                with horror"?
Response 2:   Horrible to whom? (or) Would *everyone* think they were
                horrible?

Identification

A healthy and effective map of the world allows for *difference*. It provides us with the flexibility to both label and categorize experiences and phenomena and to leap logical levels of thought. *Identification* on the other hand is a complex process by which we *confuse* one action with a specific response (anchoring the two in our mind) so that one not only *leads* to the other (cause–effect), but *is* the other (complex equivalence). While this is important in our early development when we learn as children to equate words (symbols) with experiences (referents), it can result in extremely impoverished maps of the world if we forget that the symbol and the referent are two different things that operate at different logical levels in reality.

An identification statement demonstrates that the speaker has adopted an equation between things on different levels of abstraction that indicate a perception of *absolute sameness*. It represents a "confusion" of the multiordinal nominalization *self* with some adjective (some word, label, definition, understanding, etc.), and this neuro-linguistic *state* is accepted as *real*. The speaker has "lost quotes" and believes the expression because he actually feels it in his body. "I'm a *patriot*" is an example of someone who identifies with the nominalized form of *patriotic*, and "I'm a *deep thinker*" with the process of *thinking deeply*. Neither of these expressions are necessarily a reflection of a dysfunctional delusion. However, the illustration below demonstrates the potentially negative power of this type of thinking.

Identification

"I'm a *rage-aholic*" (*identification*) or "He is such a *nerd*" (*predication* – projecting an internal judgment or value to something outside the speaker) are additional examples of this neuro-semantic process that are likely to limit or cause the speaker pain as in the illustration above. By using "to be" verbs (is, am, are, was, were, be, being, been, etc.) to lock in the identity to the word, the speaker has created a reified map of the world and trapped himself within the model. When we *identify*, we create a mental illusion (or delusion or hallucination) of reality. As exemplified in the above illustration, such a reified map of the world can be self-perpetuating.

There are several appropriate steps to take to assist the speaker to recognize the trap he or she is in and lead them to more options.

Speaker: I'm stupid.
Response: (Extensionalize by adding referents to the deleted process)
              How does this one action make you "stupid"? Does this
              mean you will still be stupid tomorrow? Were you stupid
              yesterday?

Speaker: He's a jerk.
Response 1:   (Extensionalize) What did he do to warrant the label "jerk"?
              Was he always a jerk? What changed?
Response 2:   (Attempt to separate and differentiate the disparate reali-
              ties) What does a "jerk" look like/sound/behave like? What
              does the "he" to whom you are referring actually look/
              sound/behave like? How are the two different?

A friend stopped by to talk about an insight he had regarding problems with anger that he had experienced for years. In a book about anger, he discovered that his problems were symptomatic of someone who had been abused as a child and, since he had suffered such abuse, this now explained *why* he had anger-control issues. "I'm *sick*," he stated matter-of-factly. This reified description of his reality is a perfect example of this process. If it is not challenged, then the following will likely accurately describe his *self-perception*: "I'm sick now. I was sick then, and I will always be sick!"

Personalizing

Personalizing occurs when we attach personal significance to the behavior and communication of others or to specific events that could just as easily be understood impersonally. A person who uses these cognitive distortions is actually regressing to the process by which infants and young children learn to associate what occurs in the world with themselves. This *egocentric* view of the world can be particularly disruptive when we assume the actions of others are targeting or attacking us, as in the illustration below. In this example, there are many possible *reasons why* she did not get a return call, only one of which is being expressed and believed.

Personalizing

Reconnecting the speaker with the actual events (*extensional* referents) while removing the perceived connection between them (the *intensional* verbal map) can be accomplished using several approaches.

Speaker: He didn't call just to get back at me.
Response 1:   (Challenge the mind reading) How do you know what his motivation was when he didn't call?
Response 2:   (Challenge the complex equivalence) Aren't there other possibilities? What if he just got stuck in a meeting?

Speaker: I'm late. Now I feel guilty for causing your special dinner to burn!

Response 1:   (Challenge the cause and effect) How could your being late *cause* the dinner to burn?

Response 2:   (Jump a meta-level and challenge the possible habitual pattern) So, since you weren't the cook, I wonder, how often do you take responsibility for things you have no control over?

Metaphors

Language uses word-symbols to represent our maps of the world and, in this way, it regularly presents us with metaphorical ways to compare what we know to what we want to learn, explain, understand, and so on. We use linguistic symbols to re-present concrete objects and phenomena, then go on to use them again to form abstract thoughts and language. As Hall says, "in thinking, perceiving, understanding, and talking we constantly find, create, and use metaphors from one experience to 'make sense' of another. The fundamental nature of metaphor 'is understanding and experiencing one kind of thing in terms of another'" (p. 225).

The problem is that, as language becomes habitual, we lose track of the fact that it is simply combinations of symbols, and we "lose quotes" and begin to believe the myths and metaphors we create. This is not necessarily bad, because the process allows us to communicate very efficiently. This is evident in some of the common cultural metaphors we adopt and begin to live by, such as, "I'm having problems *getting* this idea *across* to you" or "I hope I haven't *wasted* the time I've *invested* in learning this!"

Metaphors help us learn and understand the world, and then convey our learnings to someone who hasn't had the specific experiences we have had. Because we create metaphors from a meta-level, we tend to focus on the content, leaving the process to work its magic at an unconscious (and therefore more influential) neuro-linguistic level. Metaphors invite the listener to "add in" or delete information and meaning based on personal experience rather than from the referents of the speaker. However, careful listening to the metaphors a speaker uses can give you insight into their perceptions, presuppositions, attitudes, and so on.

Speaker: I don't know if I can *bear this burden* much longer!
Response 1:   How do you experience *carrying* the burden? What is its *weight* like? Do you feel you must *bear* it alone?
Response 2:   (Help the speaker to expand on the concept of *burden*) What is it you are carrying around? What makes it so heavy? What would happen if you put it down or gave it to someone else?

Summary: The Meta Model Reframed

Now that you have learned the Meta Model, here is a brief summary of the model in terms of basic Meta Model response questions.

Gathering Information

1. Who, what, where, when, how, specifically?

Use: When information is left out of the speaker's SS (deleted) or when it has been unspecified or generalized.

Example: When the speaker says, "I'm depressed," ask, "What is depressing you? What are you depressed about?"

Example: When the speaker says, "Everyone's against me," ask, "Who specifically is against you?"

Example: When the speaker says, "My love for her gets me in trouble," ask, "How specifically does loving her get you in trouble? What specifically do you do that causes problems?"

2. Can you say that about yourself?

Use: When the speaker says something about another person that may apply to himself.

Example: When the speaker says, "She never seems to understand me," ask, "Can you say 'I never seem to understand her'?"

Example: When the speaker says, "My boss hates me," say, "What do you experience when you say, 'I hate my boss'?"

Expanding Limits

3. What stops you? What would happen if you did? (catastrophic expectations)

Use: When you hear words like "can't" or "should."

Example: When the speaker says, "I can't love," ask, "What stops you from loving?"

Example: When the speaker says, "I must be understanding," ask, "What would happen if you weren't?"

4. Can you think of a time (situation) when you did (didn't)?

Use: When the speaker indicates the belief that there are *no* exceptions.

Example: When the speaker says, "Everyone thinks I'm stupid," ask, "Can you tell me one person who doesn't? You mean *everyone* thinks you're stupid, even your pet rock?"

Example: When the speaker says, "I'm always late," ask, "Can you think of a time when you weren't late?"

Changing Meanings

5. How do you know?

Use: When the speaker is mind reading.

Example: When the speaker says, "I know he doesn't love me," ask, "How do you know?"

Example: When the speaker says, "He should know better," ask, "How should he know?"

Example: When the speaker says, "She wrote it just to rekindle the fight," ask, "How do you know why she wrote it?"

6. How do they (you) make you (them) feel that way?

Use: When the speaker's statement implies cause–effect relationships with others' emotions.

Example: When the speaker says, "She makes me angry," ask, "How does she make you angry?"

Example: When speaker says, "I feel bad for making her unhappy," ask, "What did you do that you believe made her unhappy?"

7. *According to whom? By what standard?*

Use: When you hear an unsubstantiated value judgment.

Example: When the speaker says, "That was a stupid thing to do," ask, "Stupid according to whom? Stupid by what standard?"

Example: When the speaker says, "His incompetence bothers me," ask, "Who believes that he is incompetent? Incompetent in what way?"

Example: When the speaker says, "It's awful," ask, "What about it is awful? Who else thinks it's awful?"

8. *Is that true about yourself?* (similar to #2)

Use: When the speaker makes a statement that indicates a causal relationship between two phenomena that are at different logical levels.

Example: When the speaker says, "She didn't care about what I said ... She didn't even look at me," say, "When you don't look at her, does that necessarily mean you don't care?"

Example: When the speaker says, "It must be that he lied. He laughed when he said it," say, "Have you ever laughed when you weren't telling a lie?"

9. *Is there another possibility or another explanation?*

Use: When the speaker indicates the belief that there are only two possibilities.

Example: When the speaker says, "Either I don't have the smarts or the looks to make it in this field," say, "What else might be getting in your way?"

Example: When the speaker says, "They're ignorant or they're incompetent," say, "What if they are just responding to something you don't know about?"

Notes to Chapter 3

1. As Gregory Bateson says in *Steps to an Ecology of Mind* (1972): "It would seem that analogic communication is in some sense more primitive than digital and that there is a broad evolutionary trend toward the substitution of digital for analogic mechanisms in higher mammals" (p. 291).

2. See Bateson (1972, pp. 289–291). Bateson does point out context markers that may signal one interpretation as being correct.

3. The form we present here is a revision of their original model. This version deletes some of the original distinctions and expands other distinctions. We highly recommend reading the original version for more information on the origins and development of the Meta Model. Of note regarding the Meta Model is the observation by Tosey and Mathison (2009) that "there is a case for saying that the development of the meta-model, indeed the groundwork behind much of NLP in the 1970s, was strongly research-based" (p. 52). The model was significantly extended by L. Michael Hall who documented nine additional distinctions in his book *Communication Magic* (2001). These distinctions are included in a special section at the end of this chapter.

4. Because of differences in the structure of different languages, some of the distinctions presented here may not apply to the native speakers of languages other than English.

5. From Noam Chomsky's *Language and Mind* (1972) comes: "we can thus distinguish the surface structure of the sentence, the organization into categories and phrases that is directly associated with the physical signal, from the underlying deep structure, also a system of categories and phrases, but with a more abstract character" (pp. 28–29). These two are related, says Chomsky, by certain formal

operations known as grammatical transformations which include the processes of generalization, deletion, and distortion.

6. We originally identified only eight Meta Model distinctions but in this revised edition decided to add complex equivalence, a distinction that was partially covered in Chapter 1. As Hall (2001) points out, from the publication of *The Structure of Magic* in 1975 through the 1990s, "charts contained as few as 8 to as many as 13 Meta-Model distinctions" (p. 150). He also notes that, although we proposed only eight distinctions, we actually defined twelve, because there are four sub-patterns listed under the referential index distinction. In addition, as Tosey and Mathison (2009) point out, Bandler and Grinder "recognized that [Milton] Erickson's use of language bore a relationship to the meta-model – Erickson appeared to be using these same patterns, but in an inverse way" (p. 72). While these hypnotic language patterns, codified as the "Milton Model," are taught at most NLP trainings as a means for communicating with a person's "unconscious mind," they are beyond the scope of this book.

7. There are additional learning aids available online. John David Hoag, for example, offers a free set of Meta Model Flashcards at http://www.nlpls.com/articles/metamodel/MetaModelFlashcards.php. This comprehensive set of cards includes all of the original Meta Model distinctions plus Hall's nine additions to the model.

8. Hall (2001) includes unspecified verbs in this category. When a speaker uses verbs in certain ways, they omit important information. "I was manipulated," for example, doesn't specify how or in what way the speaker was manipulated. Likewise with "I'm uncomfortable," where an appropriate Meta Model response would be: "In what way are you uncomfortable?"

9. This concept of a recursive relationship is echoed by Tosey and Mathison (2007). In their discussion of second-order cybernetics, they point out that "in any interaction between a coach and their client, the coach is involved in a recursive engagement within that system … The coach is not able simply to 'reprogramme' the client, because he or she is part of the 'programme' that is running in the interaction" (p. 95).

10. Hoag, an NLP trainer, coach and therapist in California provides a comprehensive overview of NLP and especially the Meta Model on his website (http://www.nlpls.com/articles/NLPmetaModel.php). In his version of the Meta Model, he makes a distinction between Modal Operators of Necessity (i.e., "must") and Modal Operators of Judgment (i.e., "should"), which is an interesting refinement of this pattern.

11. Double bind theory was an area explored by Gregory Bateson in his work with cybernetics in the 1950s. Therapeutic double binds are created when the practitioner provides the client with an illusion of choice where either selection will result in the same positive outcome. Utilizing a speaker's own universal quantifier in a therapeutic double bind can create the "Aha!" experience and provide a little levity to the session.

12. On his website (http://www.nlpls.com/articles/NLPmetaModel. php), Hoag has a comment regarding this Meta Model violation that is insightful: "Some Meta Model violations, it should be noted, can be the result, rather than the cause, of other limiting patterns. 'Mind reading,' for example, is not necessarily linguistically originated but is, instead, often the linguistic representation of self/other identity confusion, boundary ambiguity and other core state meta patterns."

13. For an elegant and pragmatic discussion of the calibrated communication cycle in families, see Bandler et al. (1976), especially Part II.

14. Hall (2001) makes a case for using "why" questions in certain situations such as intentional why (Why do you want that?); value why (Why is that so important to you?); explanation why (Why do you hold it that way?); and causation or source why (Why do think it's awful?). See his explanation starting on p. 155.

Chapter 4

The Visual Model

It soon became very obvious that good spellers had a very consistent strategy and accompanying set of accessing cues. The vast majority of them tended to look up and to their left while searching for the spelling. According to NLP this indicates an accessing strategy of remembered visual imagery (V^r).

Robert Dilts, "The NLP Spelling Strategy"

It was Bandler and Grinder's (1975) remarkable observation that a person's use of certain predicates – those that evoke specific representational systems – along with the way they moved their eyes that gave them the ability to identify and map a person's mental *strategies*. These strategies included how individuals came to conclusions, made decisions, or how they prevented themselves from feeling, thinking, and behaving in ways that would enrich their lives. In this chapter we will focus on *eye accessing cues*, one of the *minimal cues* that we can use to help us understand how a person is retrieving internal memories and making sense of the world. With this information, we can both gain rapport with and assist individuals who want to experience some change in their lives.

Pupil Response

In the early 1960s there appeared on the market a unique type of sunglasses. They were very much like a one-way mirror: the wearer could comfortably see out, much like ordinary shaded glasses, but no one could see in through their mirror-like reflection. They quickly gained in popularity and soon were given the colloquial name "cheaters."

The significance of that name lies in the profound intuitive awareness we have of the importance of our eyes in communication. Some people are more alert than others to what is communicated by the eyes. In his discussion with Kenneth Friedman on Middle Eastern cultures, Hall observes that the Arabs have known about pupil response for years. This unconscious response is an *emotional indicator*. "Since people can't control the response of their eyes, which is a dead giveaway, many Arabs ... wear dark glasses, even indoors" (Friedman, 1979, pp. 47–48).

Desmond Morris also addresses this phenomenon in his book *Manwatching*: "the jade dealers of pre-Revolutionary China ... took to wearing dark glasses expressly in order to hide their excited pupil dilations when they were handed a particularly valuable specimen of jade."[1] Especially important in Western cultures where the "look-to-listen" rule is so widespread, our eyes play a critical part in communicative processes.

The Visual System

This diagram of the visual system shows how visual input is transmitted by the optic nerve to the brain. Notice how portions of the input from the right and left fields of vision go to opposite sides of the brain. This crossover occurs at a junction called the optic chiasma.

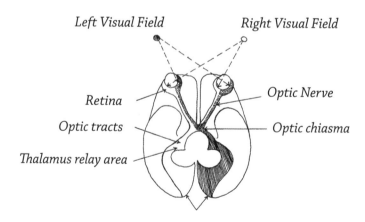

Left Visual Field   Right Visual Field

Retina   Optic Nerve

Optic tracts   Optic chiasma

Thalamus relay area

Occipital Cortex

Visual sensations may be generated by stimulation other than light, such as pressure on the eyeball and electric stimulation of certain parts of the brain.

It is the sympathetic division of the autonomic nervous system (ANS) that acts to change pupil size in response to emotional stimulation. Even conditions of mild arousal or interest will systematically affect the pupil. Knowing what emotional states elicit these systematic changes can give the astute observer a special kind of "insight" into a person's internal state.

Eckhard Hess (1975) began to study pupil dilations as a psychologist at the University of Chicago. His research stimulated a great deal of interest in "expressive eyes," showing that pupil dilation or constriction is an extremely accurate indicator of that person's response to stimulation.[2] Results demonstrated that when a person is interested or aroused, the pupil dilates. When confronted with unpleasant or noxious stimuli, the pupil constricts.

Ocular Accessing Cues

When someone is trying to "remember" something, part of what you see, if you watch closely, are specific patterns of movement and changes in the person's physiology related to the process of remembering. As you read the following examples, imagine that you are closely watching the people described.

> Rita told us that she was confused. She sat for a long moment with her head bowed, and she shook it slowly from side to side. Finally, gazing down at the floor to her left, she muttered, "Somehow, it just doesn't feel right."

From Rita's words, you can easily guess that she is very much into her feelings. However, there is another piece of important information given by *just her eyes alone*.

> As if the ceiling behind me could somehow give him the answer, he searched intently back and forth over my brow, saying, "Let me see now."

This person's words provide one immediate clue: he is somehow visually "searching" for information. And again we are presented with analog gestures that are just as informative as the words: what he is doing with his eyes.

In the mid-1970s Bandler and Grinder began to study the patterns of movements of people's eyes as they thought and spoke. They discovered that these movements correlated fairly well with certain types of *information retrieval behaviors*. These systematic patterns of behavior were eventually formalized into a model called *accessing cues*.[3] More recently labeled the eye accessing cues (EAC) model, there has been some research into the validity of this model (see "Research Notes" below).

Eye-Scanning Patterns

When people are thinking and talking, they move their eyes in what is known as *eye-scanning patterns*.[4] These movements appear to be symptomatic of their attempts to gain access to internally stored or internally generated information. This information is encoded in our minds in one or more of the representational systems (see Chapter 2). When a person "goes inside" to retrieve a memory or to create a new thought, he exhibits certain behaviors indicative of the representational system he is accessing at that moment. The two examples given above demonstrate these accessing behaviors in action.

Split-Brain Theory: Two-in-One

Split-brain studies at the California Institute of Technology during the 1950s and 1960s opened up a whole new field of brain research. Under the direction of Roger Sperry, a Caltech group conducted research on patients whose epileptic seizures had been controlled by an operation that severed the corpus callosum and related commissures. This procedure isolated one cerebral hemisphere from the other by severing the communication pathways between them.[5]

Major results of the research indicated a *hemispheric specialization*. Each hemisphere of the brain apparently employs different modes of processing information (see diagram below). It is possible that this specialization of brain function is being emulated by a person's eye-scanning movements when he is thinking and calling upon different portions of the brain to process information.

The following list of words from Joseph Bogen (1975) indicates parallel ways of "knowing."[6] The illustration represents the two hemispheres of the brain and the bilateral crossover that is most obvious as "handedness." A right-handed person has a dominant left-hemisphere; a left-handed person has a dominant right-hemisphere.

LEFT HEMISPHERE		*RIGHT HEMISPHERE*
intellect		*intuition*
convergent		*divergent*
digital		*analogic*
secondary		*primary*
abstract		*concrete*
directed		*free*
propositional		*imaginative*
analytic		*holistic*
linear		*nonlinear*
rational		*intuitive*
sequential		*multiple*
objective		*subjective*
successive		*simultaneous*

Eye-scanning patterns are the most easily observable accessing behavior. The descriptions that follow are based on patterns usually exhibited by right-handed people (left-hemisphere dominant). The patterns may be reversed for *some* left-handed individuals. Please notice that this is another generalized model. It is advisable where possible to check out your observations by direct questioning and by correlating eye patterns with other accessing behaviors. See also the section on "Mapping" below.

Some Research Notes: A Slight Detour

NLP has been in something of a Catch-22; it is dismissed because it is said that there is no evidence for it, yet there is no evidence for it at least in part because research is not being done, and research is not being done because the field is dismissed. Why? Because there is no evidence to support it.

Paul Tosey and Jane Mathison, "Fabulous Creatures of HRD"

Both accessing cues and preferred representational systems (PRS) covered in Chapter 2 are NLP constructs that received significant attention and became focal areas for research during the late 1970s and through the early 1990s. Most researchers were attempting to validate the link between predicate usage and visual accessing cues and the existence of a PRS. Diamantopoulos et al. (2009) have analyzed a number of these studies. While they report that "a clear conclusion as to the validity of the model has not been reached" (p. 9), they go on to describe how difficulties in the research stemmed in part from unrefined definitions of *transderivational search*, the process by which subjects access the meaning of questions or verbal instructions from the researchers. This observation will have special significance when we discuss the process of *mapping* accessing cues later in this chapter.

There have been several other reviews of NLP research (e.g., Sharpley, 1984, 1987, 1987; Heap, 1988) in which the conclusions were that the research did not substantiate either the accessing cues or the PRS models. To his credit, Sharpley also observed: "This does not necessarily reduce NLP to worthlessness for counseling practice. Rather, it puts NLP in the same category as psychoanalysis, that is, with principles not easily demonstrated in laboratory settings but, nevertheless, strongly supported by clinicians in the field" (1987, p. 105).

Other reviews of the literature have presented a slightly different view. Einspruch and Forman (1985) pointed out six categories of design and methodological errors, including unfamiliarity with NLP and inadequate interviewer training. These writers took exception to the findings of Sharpley (1984) which actually resulted in his 1987 "rebuttal." More recently, Diamantopoulos et al. (2009) looked at ten studies that specifically tested the eye accessing cues and found similar flaws in the studies. However, both of these reviews identified studies demonstrating correlations in related areas of research, and both strongly suggested the need for further research related to NLP and provided suggestions for preventing the kinds of problems experienced by researchers in the studies they reviewed.

Eye Accessing Cues Schematic

When you observe people talking or thinking, you may notice their eyes constantly in motion, darting back and forth, up and down, occasionally glancing at objects and people but just as often "focused" on inner experiences. As previously mentioned, these movements are symptomatic of the way they are thinking. In the descriptions that follow, the word "looking" refers to the movement of a person's eyes in the direction indicated. "Left" means towards *that* person's left, and "right" means towards *his* right. It is helpful to keep in mind that this accessing behavior represents "looking" internally. That is, during the moment of information retrieval, people are generally *not* conscious of external visual stimuli. Rather, they are concentrating on internally stored or internally generated images, sounds, words, and feelings. The italicized words below indicate the kind of information being accessed.

- **Looking up and to the right:** *Constructed images.* These are visual images or pictures that are created by the individual. They can be re-combinations of pieces of previously experienced visual input (see "eidetic images" below) into new or novel forms or sequences, or they can be created images that are constructed in response to other sensory stimuli. Constructed images are usually characterized by flatness or lack of depth and sometimes by a lack of color.

- **Looking up and to the left:** *Eidetic images.* These are stored visual images or pictures of past events and other previously experienced visual stimuli. This includes dreams and constructed images that have already been experienced. These images are usually characterized by having both depth and motion – as in a movie – as well as color.

- **Looking level and to the right:** *Constructed speech.* This pattern is usually associated with the process of creating spoken language. In this position, the person is "putting into words" what he wants to say next.

- **Looking level and to the left:** *Remembered sound.* This includes such tonal representation as the "alphabet tune" and letters, advertisement jingles, phone numbers, and colloquialisms like slang and swearing. This is also where a person often moves the eyes when remembering *auditory tape loops*: messages stored in short, often tuneful or rhythmic patterns that have been so often repeated that the person has lost conscious awareness of their existence. One example of this is the "Remember-to-get-the-milk-on-the-way-home-from-work" line that is recited so often during the course of the morning that it eventually drops from conscious awareness.

Note: The next two eye-scanning patterns may be reversed in both right- and left-handed people. It is important to determine which pattern is being used by an individual (see "Mapping" below) before you can use the information gained from observing these eye movements.

- **Looking down and to the right:** *Feelings.* In this position a person can access both derived feelings (emotions) and stored kinesthetic memories. Think of the position you often see a depressed person in: head bowed, shoulders rounded, body drawn into itself. That person is really "into his feelings." Remember that for some individuals, accessing feelings will be down and to the left.

- **Looking down and to the left:** *Internal dialog.*[7] Usually associated with "deep thought," these are the words and sounds made internally that accompany this process. (At times these sounds and exclamations may "leak" out without a person's being aware of it. "Please stop mumbling to yourself" is an often heard response to this leakage.) Typically, internal dialog is a running commentary on your current experience. At quieter moments, it can be an analytic tool of complex, rational, logical thinking. (This would be "rational" and "logical" only relative to the individual's model of reality, not necessarily to a general consensus of reality!) This accessing pattern may be down and to the right for some individuals.[8]

- **Defocused eyes:** *Visualization.* This may be in any of the above positions and is very often used during face-to-face conversations by individuals who communicate using the "look-to-listen" rule. This is usually accessing of either eidetic or constructed visual imagery. However, it may also indicate accessing of other forms of information. When in doubt, check it out!

- **Closed eyes:** *Taste and smell.* Although people often close their eyes in order to remember a particular taste or smell, watch for movements of the eyes under the lids. These movements can indicate any of the previously discussed accessing cues and can be interpreted as if the eyes were open. The following illustrations demonstrate how the eye positions appear to the observer. Put together, they form the eye accessing cues schematic.

Looking up and to the right:
Constructing images

Looking up and to the left:
Remembering images

Looking level and to the right:
Constructing speech

Looking level and to the left:
Remembering sounds

*Looking down and
to the right:*
Feelings

*Looking down and
to the left:*
Internal dialog

Note: This schematic may be reversed in some left-handed people.

Caution: This represents a *generalization* of human behavior.

Remember: When in doubt, check it out!

Other Accessing Patterns

Breathing

There are other observable behaviors – what Dilts and DeLozier call "micro behavioural cues" (2000, p. 1099) – associated with accessing patterns. *Breathing*, for example, can be an excellent indicator of certain information retrieval patterns. Often when people are accessing visually, either constructing an image or remembering eidetic images, their breathing becomes very shallow. It can even stop altogether! The following recounting of a therapy session demonstrates how this kind of information can be useful.

The therapist has noticed that when the husband (Joe) faces his wife, there are often long pauses in his breathing. At particularly stressful times he even holds his breath. Joe has just indicated that whenever his wife looks at him "a particular way" he feels upset (see "Complex Equivalence," in Chapter 3).

> Therapist: Would you tell me, Joe, how your wife's looking at you that way causes you to be upset?[9]

Joe's immediate non-verbal response to the question is to glance up and to his left. As he does so, his breathing almost stops, and there is a long pause before he speaks. This matches the behavior previously observed by the therapist.

> Joe: I don't know. I just get the idea she's disgusted or angry with me or something.

From Joe's analog response, the therapist has a very important and potentially useful piece of information. His behavior indicates a strong possibility that Joe is "seeing" an internal image from some past experience (an eidetic image). When Joe "sees" this image, he becomes upset. It is important to note that Joe is completely unaware of this process ("I don't know. I just get the idea ...")

If this is true, then it is not actually his wife's looking at him that "certain way" which is upsetting him. It is, rather, some visually coded memory that is elicited or brought to mind by that look. In effect, Joe is responding to an *internally generated* experience (see pages 27–29) rather than to the externally presented stimuli. After determining from Joe that his wife is still looking at him "that way," the therapist's intervention demonstrates how a slight change in Joe's behavior can have a dramatic effect on his experience.

> Therapist: Joe, I wonder if you could look at your wife again, and as you do, I would like you to do two things: I want you to continue to look at her rather than looking away and, as you

look at her, I want you to take several slow deep breaths. Will you do that?

Joe: Uh, sure, I guess so.

As he carries out the therapist's instructions, Joe experiences a moment of confusion, but as it passes, he comments: "Say, you know I didn't feel that way this time!" A portion of the remaining session was devoted to instructing Joe on how and when he could use this "new behavior" to help him achieve his goal of "better communication" with his wife.

Body Posture

Body posture can also be a good indicator of how a person is accessing information. It is much easier to "visualize" when you assume a "visual's" posture: back straight and erect, chin raised and forward, eyes looking up, and breathing shallow. To access feelings, round the shoulders and back, lean forward, and breathe deeper into the abdomen. Taking the "telephone" posture – with the head tilted to one side – we can facilitate tonal information accessing, while the arms-folded, head back posture of the "digital" is a good way to become digitalized.

Minimal Cues

Often people will exhibit very slight shifts or variations from their "normal" stature. These behaviors are *minimal cues*. By training yourself to be alert to these slight shifts, you can often catch subtle nuances of communication that pass most people by at the conscious level.

Auditory accessing is often simply a slight tilt of the head as the person recalls "tape loops" (often-repeated self-messages) or tries to remember what someone has said. Deep thought utilizing internal dialog looks much like Rodin's famous sculpture of *The Thinker*, with various personal modifications. A slight stiffening of the spine or tensing of the shoulders can indicate visual processing, while the opposite minimal cues – rounded shoulders and curved spine – can indicate that a person is "getting in touch" with the information.

Going through the Motions

Have you ever walked into a room and then, having forgotten what it was that you were after, found yourself retracing your steps in order to remember? What you are doing is literally placing your body back into physical positions that will help you remember. (Of course, visual and other cues along the way also help.) Often, in order to accurately describe a particular complex motion, like a golf swing or tennis serve, the person giving the description will find himself literally going through the motions. These are both examples of a special case of kinesthetic accessing involving movement. As you become more alert to the minimal cues people give as they communicate, you will notice people's muscles involuntarily responding with subtle movements as they recall the gross motor movements of the actions they are accessing.

Mapping

Mapping is a process by which you can determine both an individual's preferred representational system and also that person's eye-scanning and other accessing behaviors. For example, with Part A (below), you can determine whether a person systematically looks down left for feelings or for internal dialog. Since accessing cues may be reversed in some left-handers, it can be important to determine which side of the visual eye-scanning pattern is eidetic imaging and which is constructed imaging. Once you know this information, you will find that it remains fairly constant for any individual. Though accessing patterns seem to remain stable in adults, children below the age of six or seven do not demonstrate patterns as consistently as children who are older. This may occur due to the continued development of hemispheric dominance before that age.

Part B of the mapping process demonstrates how a person is responding to the environment at that particular moment and may also indicate habitual patterns of information accessing. With this information, you can discern a person's preferred representational system and representational system hierarchy. Remember, however, that these can change depending on such variables as setting, the amount of stress the individual is experiencing, and his or her response to you.

Mapping may be used to simply verify the meaning of one small piece of behavior or information. In the example where Joe exhibited the analog behavior of glancing up and to the left, the therapist could verify that he was "seeing" an eidetic image by simply asking the appropriate mapping question. Or you can map a person completely prior to a formal counseling session. Mapping can be done overtly, or the questions can be embedded in the course of an ordinary interview. Eventually, as you "tune" yourself to the people around you, you may find that the process of mapping people becomes an automatic part of your own communicative behavior. Done in this way, almost unconsciously, it can be a tremendously useful means of both gathering important information and gaining rapport.

Accessing Cue Sequences

It is important to understand that the response to a question to evoke a specific representational system cue can instead trigger a sequence of accessing cues. These clusters of behavior may indicate the "circuitous" strategy the individual used to access the specific experience asked for. For example, if you ask for a remembered image, such as, "What color was your first car?" you would expect the person to glance up and to the left. However what you could get is a sequence of accessing cues: the individual might first close his eyes briefly, flare his nostrils, then look down and right, take a deep breath, then look up and left and finally down and to the left before responding "Metallic blue!"

Asked to recount what he just experienced, he might respond: "When you asked the question, I first remembered the smell of my car when I first bought it and then the feel of the leather seats. When I rembered how it looked, I also remembered that I need to send in my current registration and told myself not to forget!"

Part A: Mapping the Accessing Cue Schematic

As you ask the questions that follow, pay attention to the person's eyes as well as to shifts in posture and breathing. Sometimes the response is so minimal it is hard to detect. If you fail to get a satisfactory response, try using a different question or go on to the next question and come back to it later. The questions given here are only examples. You can be creative and generate questions of your own, but pay attention to the predicates you use. If they presuppose a representational system that is different from the one you are testing, the person may be led into the accessing pattern associated with that system.

1. *Constructed images.* Ask a visual question about the future, like, "What do you imagine (I, this town, that tree) will look like ten years from now?" This requires the person to construct an image of something he has not yet experienced.

2. *Eidetic images.* Ask a visual question about the past like, "What color was your first car?" or about specific information like, "How many windows are there on the front of your house?" This calls to mind some previously experienced image.

3. *Constructed speech.* Ask for a complex verbal response like, "What does it mean to be 'predisposed'?" If you preface this question with the instruction, "Just think about what you would say without answering," you allow for the "rehearsal" of speech.

4. *Remembered sounds.* Ask for auditory recall from the recent past or from a well-rehearsed "tape loop" like, "What was the first question I asked you?" or "What letter comes before P in the alphabet?"

5. *Feelings.* Ask a question that presupposes the kinesthetic system, especially derived feelings like, "How did you feel on the day before your last birthday?" or "What is the most (exciting, scary, happy) experience you have ever had?" Again, asking the person to simply think of the experience without verbally responding may give you a better analog response.

6. *Internal dialog.* Often the most difficult to detect, this cue is best observed as it naturally occurs, usually when a person is not being required to interact with others. Sometimes this cue can be elicited

by asking questions such as, "During the quieter moments in your life, what do you find yourself thinking about?"

It is important to note that people will often *lead* with the accessing pattern that is most comfortable to them. A "visual," for example, may first access with a visual accessing pattern when asked to say what letter comes before the letter P in the alphabet. What he is doing is using a visual *lead system* to create an image of the alphabet in order to answer the question. When a person persists in using one of the accessing patterns as the initial step in gaining the information, it may take several questions of the same type before you can observe the accessing cue for which you are testing.

One thing that can assist you in eliciting the pattern you are testing for is to *model* the posture, tonality, and other minimal cues that match the communication category and representational system presupposed by the question you are asking. For example, when asking a kinesthetic question, rounding your shoulders slightly, bending forward, speaking somewhat lower, and using a "placating" palm-up hand gesture may help direct the person's attention at an unconscious level to that accessing pattern.

Part B: Mapping the Preferred System and Hierarchy

In the following sections you will again be watching for accessing cues – eye movements, shifts in breathing and posture, and other indications of systematic use of *information retrieval behaviors*. Since it is important in the sections that follow to know what a person's typical accessing patterns are – whether down-left or down-right for feelings, for example – it is necessary to have already mapped the person's accessing cues schematic (see Part A). As you observe how a person responds in each of the sections below, you will be able to identify both his preferred representational system and his representational system hierarchy. As in Part A, the wording of the instructions given is only representative of what could be said. Use your own ideas in creating the instructions and questions that will be most compatible with your normal way of communicating.

Section I

Give these instructions before proceeding with the three steps below: "I'm going to say a few words, and I want you to listen to them, think about them, and be sure that you know what they mean. You don't have to tell me anything. Just listen and understand. Are you ready?"

1. *Concrete noun.* Say a concrete noun like "dog," "tree," or "boat," then pause and observe the non-verbal response as the person hears and makes sense of what he has heard. These responses will be so fast and subtle that it will require your utmost attention.

    What you are watching for is an accessing pattern. For example, upon hearing the word "dog," a "kino" might look down and to the right as he accesses the feelings associated with his understanding of what the word "dog" represents to him. A "visual" might glance up and to the left, creating an image of a dog associated with his understanding, while a "tonal" or "digital" may glance from one side to the other, repeating the word "dog" and associating it with other auditory elements. Watch for consistent use of one of these patterns as you continue below.

2. *Abstract noun.* Say an abstract noun – a nominalization like "friend-ship" or "manifestation" – then wait for the non-verbal response. The responses will usually be almost immediate.

3. *Nonsense syllables.* Say a nonsense word like, "termonacar" or "fruce-rah" (be inventive!), then pause and wait for the response. This technique is particularly effective because in order to make sense of what he has heard, the person must draw upon information from his own model of the world. You have disrupted his expectations by saying a word that doesn't make sense, and the confusion that results from the surprise nonsense syllables creates a mildly stressful situation in which he will most likely retreat to his preferred system in order to make sense of what he has just experienced.

Section II

Give these instructions prior to the next two steps: "I'm going to ask you to think about some things you may have experienced or you might experience, but I won't ask you to describe them to me. Just think about them. Ready?"

1. *Past event.* "Can you remember your last (birthday, vacation, fun weekend)?" By asking the person to draw on his experience in a general way using the unspecified verb "remember," you allow him to recall the experience in the way that is most comfortable to him, usually his preferred representational system. Again, allow time for the person to fully respond before going on to the next question.

2. *Future event.* "Where do you think you will be living ten years from now?" Notice the use of the non-sensory-specific word "think." Observe which system the person uses in order to create the response to this question.

Section III
This final section requires some spontaneity on your part as well as attention to what you *do* and *say*: they will be different! Your goal will be to determine which of two simultaneously presented *incongruent* (different) *messages* is received by the person you are working with. This will give you the person's representational system hierarchy. Study these examples closely and practice them before trying them out. Notice that each step has two parts, "Say" and "Do," which overlap as indicated.

1. *Auditory/visual incongruence*

   Say: "I'm going to ask you to pay attention to your internal experience while we do (see *Do* below) two things."

   Do: As you say the word "two" above, hold up *three* fingers for just a moment, then put them down. Do this casually and, after a few moments, ask the person, "What was the first thing you were aware of as I spoke a moment ago?"

   The person's response to the question will indicate whether he was more alert to the auditory portion of the experience or to the visual portion. If he points out the incongruity between what you said and what you did, he scores visual over auditory.

2. (a) *Kinesthetic/auditory incongruence*

   Say: "Pay attention to your thoughts as I touch you on your right (see "Do" below) knee."

160

Do: As you say the word "right", reach out and gently touch the person on his *left* knee. This is especially effective if you maintain the person's visual contact with your face, rather than with your hand. Do this by watching the person's face as you are speaking and reaching over to touch his knee. When you are through ask, "What were you aware of as I touched you a moment ago?" If the person detects the incongruity, he scores kinesthetic over auditory.

(b) *Visual/kinesthetic incongruence*

Say: "Tell me what you are aware of as I do (see "Do" below) this."

Do: As you say the word "this," with one hand gently touch the person, while with the other hand "scribe an arc" across the person's field of vision. Again, this will indicate where the person's attention is drawn. Their response will let you know how to score.

The astute reader will realize that we have left out the digital representational system from the above hierarchy testing process. The following observations may help to round out this process:

• A "digital" will be more likely to score auditory and visual over kinesthetic.

• However, a "digital" will also tend to score visual over auditory, while an "auditory" will tend to score auditory over visual.

In any event, it is important to take into consideration all aspects of a person's communicative output. The mapping skills described above are only one of the ways to facilitate understanding and determine which system of communication to use in order to obtain the rapport and trust necessary for influential communication. For more on identifying a person's hierarchy see Appendix B.

Summary

The visual model provides us with a format for seeing, understanding, and utilizing consistent patterns of observable behavior. Based in part on research and pragmatic applications of Bandler and Grinder's observations in their first two books (1975, 1976), these techniques provide quick and efficient means for determining the representational system being used by an individual at any particular moment.

Pupil response is a very accurate indicator of interest or arousal. With good light, pupil response can be seen from as far away as five feet or more. Close observation of a person's eyes during the uttering of key words or phrases can assist you in determining his areas of concern and interest. As both the jade dealers and the Arabs have realized, this response cannot be controlled, since it is governed by the sympathetic nervous system.

Eye scanning patterns or eye accessing cues also provide information about how an individual is thinking. Combined with breathing and postural shifts, they can prove to be extremely useful to both observe and utilize when working with people to discover and change limiting and pain producing behaviors. As in the earlier example, where Joe created uncomfortable feelings from an unconscious eidetic image, these behaviors usually operate outside a person's awareness and control.

The mapping process can assist you in determining the meaning of certain patterns of behavior. Part A is designed to help you identify the specific eye motion associated with each type of thinking. Sections I and II of Part B give you information about what representational system(s) a person habitually uses (the preferred representational system), and Section III shows you how to examine a person's representational system hierarchy.

By knowing a person's preferred system, you can more easily facilitate the rapport and trust important to effective communication. Knowing a person's representational system hierarchy can help you to understand how people systematically delete certain aspects of experience from their awareness and what those aspects of the environment are most likely to be. With this information, you can help people become alert to situations in which they consistently stop themselves from seeing, feeling, or hearing input. As was demonstrated by Sharon in Chapter 1 and the fire victim in Chapter 2, the deletion of portions of experience from a person's model of the world is potentially harmful and limiting to a positive and healthy life.

These mapping techniques can be used at any time during the course of an interview, therapy session, or any setting where verbal communication is taking place. The important thing to remember is to maintain continuity and rapport. To suddenly turn to someone and say, "Can you tell me the color of your first car?" may be much less effective than casually, during the course of a conversation, mentioning an anecdote about your first car. Then you can say, "You know, I don't even remember what color it was ... Do you remember the color of *your* first car?"

People access all the time. Once you get used to the concept and its uses you will find that it is usually unnecessary to go through the formal mapping process. Many people will give you all the information you need during the course of a normal conversation.

Finally, above all else, this chapter is about learning to utilize your own sensory system to observe those with whom you interact, whether as a parent, teacher, counselor, coach, supervisor, and so on. By learning to pay exquisite attention to the verbal and non-verbal signals being sent by those with whom you are communicating, you will be more effective at achieving your *intentions* as a communicator. In addition, by understanding your own tendencies, you can be alert to situations and patterns where you are prone to delete or ignore signals that can be important to understanding and working with people.

Notes to Chapter 4

1. See the chapter "Pupil Signals" in Morris (1977), beginning on p. 169, which is an excellent and stimulating resource for anyone interested in human behavior.

2. See Hess' book *The Tell-Tale Eye* (1975) for a complete description of this phenomenon.

3. See Bandler and Grinder (1979, pp. 22–27).

4. While recent research on non-visual gaze patterns (NVGPs) (e.g., Erhlichman et al., 2007; Micic et al., 2010) demonstrates a link between eye movements and non-visual cognitive activities, there are still questions about the validity of the model that follows. The reader is strongly encouraged to review the research previously cited and to follow developments as reported in Current Research in NLP and other relevant journals.

5. For more information, see Sperry et al. (1969).

6. See Bogen (1975).

7. For a fascinating discussion on the nature of internal dialog, see Donald Meichenbaum's *Cognitive Behavior Modification* (1977).

8. Interestingly, Dilts and DeLozier (2000) define the downward eye accessing cues slightly differently: "Eyes down accompany feeling. An eye position to the left hand side is often indicative of memory, while a movement to the right side indicates imagination" (p. 1099). While the description we have presented in the current text coincides with our observations, this is one of those areas ripe for research.

9. Notice the therapist's intentional use of the cause and effect pattern here. In this way he paces Joe's experience and uses the pattern to ensure good rapport. This utilization of a Meta Model violation is an effective out-of-awareness means of operating within the client's model of the world in a way which enhances the trust important to therapeutic communication. Asking in this way also elicits an uninhibited demonstration of the dysfunctional pattern that is preventing the client from being able to change. The observant therapist can utilize this piece of the client's model of the world in very productive ways as the session continues.

Appendix A: Constraints On Our Models of the World

The diagram below illustrates the three constraints that affect the construction of our models of the world. As discussed in Chapter 1, we start with the "raw materials" of experience. These are channeled via our sensory organs through our *neurological filters*. At any moment in time, we have available to us one complete 4-tuple which includes an experience of sight, feeling, sound, and taste and smell.

From there, our experience is further modified by language and other *social filters* that either enhance our perception or diminish it.

Finally, our great body of stored memories creates an *individual filter* which further modifies our perception, sometimes by heightening and other times by obscuring the original sensory data. This internally generated experience can take the place of any of the four parameters of the 4-tuple at any moment in time. The completed 4-tuple with its combination of experiences of external and internal origins is then shuttled into memory, where it may be called upon to modify future experiences as they arise.

Appendix B: The Representational System _ _ _ _ Test

For each of the following statements, place the number 4 next to the phrase that best describes you, 3 next to the phrase that would next best describe you, and so on, ending with a 1 next to the phrase that least describes you. Do this for each of the five statements. Scoring information follows the test.

1. I make important decisions based on:

— gut level feelings

— which way sounds the best

— what looks best to me

— precise diligent study of the issues

2. During an argument, I am most likely to be influenced by:

— the other person's tone of voice

— whether or not I can see the other person's point of view

— the logic of the other person's argument

— whether or not I feel I am in touch with the other person's true feelings

3. I most easily communicate what is going on with me by:

— the way I dress

— the feelings I share

— the words I choose

— my tone of voice

4. It is easy for me to:

— find the ideal volume and tuning on a stereo system

— select the most intellectually relevant points concerning an interesting subject

— select superbly comfortable furniture

— select rich color combinations

5. Rate the following from most (4) to least (1) like you.

— I am very attuned to the sounds in my surroundings

— I am very adept at making sense of new facts and data

— I am very sensitive to the way articles of clothing feel on my body

— I have a strong response to colors and the way a room looks

Scoring the Representational System Bias Test

Step 1: Copy the answers from the test onto the lines below.

1. _____ A

_____ A

_____ V

_____ D

2. _____ A

_____ V

_____ D

_____ K

3. _____ V

_____ K

_____ D

_____ A

4. _____ A

_____ D

_____ K

_____ V

5. _____ A

_____ D

_____ K

_____ V

Note: Obviously, a test as brief as this will not give absolutely accurate data on an individual. However, as a quick and easy tool for identifying potential problems, strengths, and weaknesses between individuals, it has proven quite useful in several settings including analysis of business management styles and in marriage and family counseling sessions. The immediate feedback and the ability to compare scores promotes healthy and productive discussion between participants.

Step 2: Add the numbers associated with each letter. There will be five entries for each letter.

	V	K	A	D
1.				
2.				
3.				
4.				
5.				
TOTALS:				
	V	K	A	D

Step 3: The comparison of the totaled scores above give the relative preference (hierarchy) for each of the representational systems.

Appendix C: The Communication Categories Model

The chart below is organized around four preferred representational systems (PRS). These are the visual system, the kinesthetic system, the auditory system, and the digital system. This chart is an abbreviated visual representation of the model as it is presented in the text. It is a highly generalized format meant to be a guide to *your own observations*. As you grow accustomed to the distinctions presented here, you will also discover and become familiar with the "interpretations" required in its use. Remember, we are all highly complex individuals, and this is only a model of certain communicative behaviors. It is a generalized, deleted, and distorted representation of those behaviors.

Pattern	"Visual"	"Kino"
Predicates which presuppose a representational system	Seems, look, bright, perspective, focus, colorful	Feel, grasp, touch, firm, warm, cool, get a handle on
Posture	Straight, erect, head and shoulders up	Curved, bowed, head and shoulders down
Body "type" and movements	Either thin or obese; tight, jerky	Soft, full, rounded, loose, flowing
Lip size	Thin, tight	Full, soft
Breathing	High in chest	Low into abdomen
Voice tonality, speed, and volume	High, clear, fast, loud	Low, airy, slow, soft

Pattern	"Visual"	"Kino"
Eye elevation in relation to others	Above others	Below others
Rule for looking while listening	"Look to listen"	Would rather touch than look
Satir category	"Warner"	"Placater"
Meta Model violations	Reversed references, modal operators of necessity	Unspecified verbs, modal operators of possibility
Meta Model ill-formed meanings	Mind reading	Cause and effect
Accessing cues	Up left and right	Down left or right

Pattern	"Tonal"	"Digital"
Predicates which presuppose a representational system	Tone, loud, rings a bell, sounds like, harmonious	Statistically speaking, reasonable, logical, know
Posture	"Telephone" posture – head tilted to side	Arms folded, erect, head up
Body "type" and movements	Inconsistent body; between tight and loose	Soft, full, rigid
Lip size	Varies	Thin, tight
Breathing	Full range	Restricted
Voice tonality, speed, and volume	Melodic, rhythmic, variable	Monotone, clipped, consistent
Eye elevation in relation to others	Often diverted down to listen	"Gazes" over others' heads
Rule for looking while listening	"Don't look to listen"	No eye contact
Satir category	"Distracter"	"Computer"
Meta Model violations	Generalized and deleted referential index	Generalized and deleted referents, nominalizations
Meta Model ill-formed meanings	Lost performative	Lost performative
Accessing cues	Level left and right (head often tilted and down)	Level left and right (head often in an up position)

Appendix D: The Meta Model Crosswalk

L. Michael Hall's Expanded Meta Model and the Meta Model Crosswalk

We recognize that there are a number of different versions of the Meta Model. What follows is our attempt to bridge the "Lewis and Pucelik" model with the popular model presented by L. Michael Hall and regularly taught at NLP trainings throughout the world. His extremely informative book, *Communication Magic* (2001), in which he discusses the background for the creation of the Meta Model from linguistic and pragmatic points of view and the rationale for his nine additional Meta Model distinctions, is the basis for this summary. While some of what follows may appear to be a repeat of material already covered, Hall's distinctions and his descriptions of the processes involved have unique variations and subtlety that differentiate them from ours.

The numbering protocol we use here comes from Hall's charts, the Meta Model of Language (2001, Chart 8.1, p. 134) and the Meta Model summary (2001, p. 137) (neither of which coincide exactly with the numbering he uses in the text). The Lewis and Pucelik (L and P) distinctions are from the Meta Model outline at the beginning of Chapter 3 in this book and also include the sub-distinctions numbered in the text.

Note: The list below includes twenty-two Meta Model *distinctions* with associated Meta Model responses (*questions* or *challenges*). As Hall points out, the distinctions are the language patterns that demonstrate a speaker's *structures* or aspects of his map (model) of the world. When we notice that these surface expressions (words, phrases, and statements) are communicating an impoverished model of the world, we can respond with the appropriate Meta Model tools: "As we *meta-model*, we invite a person to reconnect to his or her *experiences* out of which the map arose and to re-map it more fully, appropriately, and usefully" (Hall, 2001, p. 183). In keeping with Hall's presentation, the model is organized using the modeling categories of deletion, generalization, and distortion.

The New and Extended Meta Model

Linguistic Distinctions of Deletion

1. Simple Deletions. This distinction occurs when the surface expression does not fully identify or overgeneralizes the referential index (the thing, object, individual, group, etc. being referred to). Identified by use of generalized words like "people," "it," or "they" and by unspecified nouns that designate categories or groups, such as "a government" or "the liberals."

Lewis and Pucelik (L and P) Distinction: I. A. 3. Generalized referential index.

2. Comparative and Superlative Deletions (or Unspecified Relations). This pattern shows up with adjectives that end in *-er* and *-est* such as "scarier," "smarter," "fastest," and so on, where the speaker fails to identify the subject that is being compared to (the missing referent or what is being related to) and/or the basis for the comparison.

L and P Distinction: III. C. Lost performative.

3. Unspecified Referential Indices (Unspecified Nouns and Verbs). This occurs when the surface expression presents a reduced version of the full experience as in, "They scare me." Here the surface structure presented by the speaker has left out important deep structure referents (objects or processes the sentence *refers* to).

L and P Distinction: I. A. 2. Unspecified referential index; I. C. Unspecified verbs.

4. Unspecified Processes (Adverbs Modifying Verbs). This pattern occurs when the speaker deletes portions of the process by using an adverb that usually ends in *-ly*. In the example, "*Surprisingly*, I understood you," the speaker both indicates a judgment while at the same time "solidifying" his state of mind–body consciousness in a way that sounds like an uncontestable fact. Other examples include "unfortunately" (mental *judgment*), "slowly" (a way of *doing* something), and "happily" (a *state* of mind).

L and P Distinction: III. C. Lost performative. (This is a specific form of LP: specifically, it is any value-laden adverb ending in *-ly* where the evaluator is not identified.)

5. Unspecified Processes (Adjectives Modifying Nouns). Certain adjectives indicate an evaluative meta-level process by which the speaker *projects* his meta-state judgment (higher-level observation) onto the noun (the *referent*). "It was an unclear presentation," for example, could mean that either the presenter was unclear or that the speaker felt unclear in his own processes of listening and interpreting, or both.

L and P Distinction: III. C. Lost performative. (This is a specific form of LP: specifically, it is any value-laden adjective where the evaluator is not identified.)

Linguistic Distinctions of Generalizations

6. Universal Quantifiers (Allness Words). This pattern is easily identifiable when the speaker uses *universal allness* terms like "every," "always," "everybody," "none," "nothing," and so on. "*Everybody* avoids me," exemplifies a severely distorted map of the world where the speaker perceives limited options, because, if it is *true*, the speaker will likely suffer from self-inflicted isolation.

L and P Distinction: II. B. Universal quantifiers.

7. Modal Operators (Operational Modes of Being). These verbally expressed *modes of operating* include necessity, desire, possibility, impossibility, and choice. "I *must* (necessity) or *want to* (desire) or *can* (possibility) or *can't* (impossibility) or *will* (choice) exercise today."

L and P Distinction: II. A. 1. Modal operators of necessity; and II A. 2. Modal operators of possibility.

8. Lost Performative (Unspecified Speakers of Map-Makers). Lost performatives are evaluative statements where the person making the evaluation or judgment (the *performer*) is not identified (deleted). As generalizations about the world, they often function as rules or principles of life and are presented as self-evident *truths*. Frequently combined with other Meta Model violations, as noted in some of the examples above, this pattern indicates a model of the world that can limit the speaker's perceived ability to take action.

L and P Distinction: III. C. Lost performative.

Linguistic Distinctions of Distortions

9. Nominalizations (Pseudo-Nouns that Hide Processes and Actions). These are *action words* that have been transformed and reified into *static concepts*. The ongoing process of "relating" becomes "relationship," and "managing" becomes "management." There is an inherent sense of finality and loss of control with these words that limit our ability to change, grow, move, and so on.

L and P Distinction: I. B. Nominalizations.

10. Mind Reading (Attributing Knowledge of Another's Internal Thoughts, Feelings, Motives). Mind-reading statements *declare*, *claim*, or *assume* knowledge of another's thoughts, emotions, values, and so on. They are created by a combination of deletions, presuppositions, and referential index shifts that show up in surface structure statements. These statements also often reflect the speaker's own feelings that have been projected onto another person.

L and P Distinction: III. A. Mind reading.

11. Cause–Effect (Causational Statements of Relations between Events, Stimulus–Response Beliefs). Here, phenomena that are easily observable in physics are distorted by applying them to complex human systems. The speaker asserts or implies that one thing necessarily leads to another. This can be particularly troublesome in relationships where one or both partners systematically delete personal responsibility for emotions. *Implied causation* is often associated with words like "that," "since," and "because" as well as the word "but." *Non-symmetrical* or one-sided descriptions of interactions can also hide cause–effect beliefs as in "He fights with me." This is different than saying, "He *attacks* me," because it excludes the speaker's reciprocal role in the action of fighting.

L and P Distinction: III. B. Cause and effect.

12. Complex Equivalences (Phenomena that Differ which Someone Equates as the Same). Complex equivalences occur when a speaker linguistically implies that two dissimilar things are equal; that is, that they mean exactly the same thing. "She won't look at me. She must be shy." In this case, there may be many reasons she won't look, only one of them being shyness. This can be especially useful to challenge when the speaker equates things that are at different logical levels, such as a behavior with an internal state, as in "He folded his arms. He's angry." These two statements are linked in a way that implies they each mean the same thing: arms folded = angry.

L and P Distinction: III. D. Complex equivalence.

13. Presuppositions (Silent Assumptions, Unspoken Paradigms). Presuppositions are deep structure conceptual understandings that must be accepted as true for a surface structure statement to make sense. They indicate a speaker's reality-organizing principles that operate as unquestioned assumptions. For example, if a speaker says, "My boss' *aloofness* is a problem," in order to make sense, the listener must assume that the boss *is aloof*. These assumptions originate in our interactions and experiences with family, culture, religion, school, and so on. Many of these presuppositions that reflect distortions of the speaker's model of the world incorporate patterns previously covered, such as cause–effect relationships, complex equivalences, and lost performatives. Presuppositions sometimes "hide" as descriptions or clauses within a statement, as in: "He's even meaner than my last boyfriend" (her last boyfriend was mean, and her current boyfriend is also mean), and they often follow verbs like "realize," "know, and "ignore" as in "I realize that she is upset" (assumes that she is upset).

L and P Distinction: None.

Extended Meta Model Distinctions

1. Over/Under Defined Terms. This Meta Model distinction comes into play when we overgeneralize and confuse our "verbal maps" with the territory (known linguistically as *intension*) while at the same time systematically under-defining important evaluative words by failing to link them to more concrete referents (known linguistically as *extension*). Examples of evaluative words are "good," "bad," "ugly," "useful," and "counterproductive" and nouns such as "marriage," "teacher," "partner," or "father" where the meaning of the word is more dependent on internally generated experience than on external see, hear, feel experiences. While this is the same process used to create fantasy, if we don't regularly perform reality checks on these assumptions we run the risk of failing to adjust ourselves to the "real" world.

L and P Distinction: Refined application of III. C. Lost performative.

2. Delusional Verbal Splits. Delusional verbal splits occur as a result of linguistic or conceptual "splintering" of reality into distinct aspects (known as *elementalism*). This can be particularly problematic when we apply this compartmentalizing to processes such as communicating and relating: "My spontaneous soul resists my tendency to want to plan ahead" or "That's the part of her I don't much like."

L and P Distinction: None.

3. Either/Or Phrases. Oversimplified either/or statements indicate a map of the world that allows for only two options for how to view, value, or respond to aspects and events of our lives. With this mindset, there is no middle ground or gray areas, no ambiguity, no "both–and" perceptions.

L and P Distinction: None.

4. Multiordinality. Multiordinality occurs when a word, such as a nominalization, can be used at multiple levels of abstraction (ordinal levels 1, 2, 3, and so on) where the meaning changes at each level but the level or dimension of abstraction is not identified. Taking the process *thinking* and changing it into *thought* for example, is the first level of this abstraction. At the second level, you can have *thoughts* about your *thoughts* or even *second thoughts* about your *thoughts*, and so on. Words such as "love," "satisfaction," "insanity," and "ethics" invite us to invent our own meanings, because they are so ambiguous, as in the example, "I hate work," because this could mean the speaker hates the *act* of working but just as well could mean he hates his *job*.

L and P Distinction: Refined application of I. B. Nominalizations.

5. Static Words. Static words occur when we take a multiordinal word (see above) and lock it with a fixed and rigid meaning, then operate as if there is no other possible meaning for the word. "*Life* sucks," is an example of this mode of thinking.

L and P Distinction: Refined application of I. B. Nominalizations.

6. Pseudo Words. Pseudo words (*fake* or *false* word symbols) are nominalized process words that are completely disconnected from any referents. The word "heat" when used as a verb (*to heat*) describes a process; however, when used as a noun, it is a fiction, because there is no actual *thing* that can be named heat. Certain words that perpetrate a fictitious model of the world simply amplify emotional perceptions of events and situations, such as "tragic," "terrible," "horrible," "awful," and so on, as in: "I just can't get over the *horrible* insults he made."

L and P Distinction: Refined application of III. C. Lost performative.

7. Identification. Identification is a complex process by which we *confuse* one action with a specific response (anchoring the two in our mind) so that one not only *leads* to the other (cause–effect), but *is* the other (complex equivalence). An identification statement creates an equation between things on different levels of abstraction, causing a "confusion" of the multiordinal nominalization *self*, as in "I'm stupid" or "He's a jerk." Using these "to be" verbs (is, am, are, was, were, be, being, been, etc.) locks the identity to the word, creating a reified map of the world and trapping the speaker within the model. When we identify, we create a mental illusion (or delusion or hallucination) of reality.

L and P Distinction: Refined application of III. C. Lost performative.

8. Personalizing. Personalizing occurs when we attach personal significance to the behavior and communication of others or to specific events that could just as easily be understood impersonally. This can be particularly disruptive when we assume the actions of others are targeting or attacking us, as in, "He didn't call just to get back at me" or "I'm late. Now I feel guilty for causing your special dinner to burn!"

L and P Distinction: Refined application of III. B. Cause and effect.

9. Metaphors. Because we use word-symbols to represent our maps of the world, we also easily use and understand language used to metaphorically represent the world. Metaphorical words help us learn and understand what we want to learn and understand, and then convey it to someone who hasn't had the specific experiences we have had. Listening to the metaphors a speaker uses can give you insight into their perceptions, presuppositions, attitudes, and so on. "I don't know if I can *bear this burden* much longer!" is a statement rich in metaphor.

L and P Distinction: None.

Glossary of Terms

The numbers in parentheses following the definitions indicate the page(s) in the text where a more complete explanation of the term may be found.

abstract noun: see "nominalization." (92)

accessing cues: movements of the eyes which are symptomatic of cerebral processes of retrieving thoughts and other experiences stored in the brain. (143–149)

analog: any form of output (behavior) exclusive of word-symbols. (78–79)

auditory tape loops: thoughts, expressions, and persistent ideas stored in short, often tuneful or rhythmic auditory patterns. (150)

calibrated communication: sometimes called a "calibrated loop," these are unconscious patterns of communication in which a look, gesture, or expression unintentionally triggers a response from another person. Often based on subliminal cues – minimal gestures that operate outside the awareness of the individuals involved – these calibrated communication loops can be the source of pain-producing miscommunication between couples, family members, and co-workers. (110)

cause and effect: a Meta Model violation in which the speaker indicates a belief that one person can directly cause another person to have a particular emotion. (112–115)

communication categories model: based on the four representational systems, this model includes the behavioral patterns associated with each of the systems (see "representational systems"). These patterns include predicate preference, posture and body type, breathing, lip size, voice tonality, eye elevation, rules for looking, Satir categories, Meta Model violations, Meta Model ill-formed meanings, and accessing cues. A complete chart of these behaviors for each system is included in Appendix C. (55–58)

complex equivalence: the relationship between a word or action and the *meaning* attached to it by the observer. It is called "complex" because the equivalent verbal description is much more detailed than the word or action being defined ("a picture is worth a thousand words"). A person's complex equivalence is a more accurate representation of his deep structure associations to the particular word or action. (introduced 31–32, and fully defined 118)

concrete nouns: see "nominalization." (92)

consensus reality: due to similarities in the neurological mechanisms within each of us and shared social and cultural experiences, we are able to create similar representations of the world called consensus reality. (7)

constraints: filters on the model-building processes. Neurological, social, and individual constraints affect our models of the world by providing experiences to be generalized, deleted, and distorted. (20–31)

deep structure (DS): the most complete linguistic representation of an experience. A person's DS is a linguistic model of his model of the world. (81)

deletion: the universal human modeling process which screens out or prevents the awareness of experiences. A primary function of the brain and central nervous system is to filter out most sensory input so that we can attend to our various activities uninterrupted. In language, deletion is the process of simplifying deep structure representations by leaving things out in the surface structure. (10)

delusional verbal splits: a Meta Model violation in which the speaker indicates a "split" or "splintered" perception of the world that is not possible and yet is limiting his ability to respond appropriately. "There is one part of me that just won't let me go along with this," is an example of a speaker who believes he is not only not "whole," but is also letting a nonexistent "part" of him guide his actions. (122)

derived feelings: see "emotions." (44)

distortion: the universal human modeling process by which we manipulate our perceptions and remembered experiences. This process often alters experiences in a way which will better fit our own models of the world, and it is also important in the creative processes of fantasizing, planning ahead, and enjoying works of art and literature. (11)

either/or phrases: this Meta Model violation presents an oversimplified model of the world in which there are only two possible realities. "Either he's mad at me or he doesn't care," indicates a speaker who has closed himself to other possibilities such as he got behind at work or some other reason for not communicating with the speaker. (123–124)

emotions: a complex set of physical sensations combined with other thought processes such as internal images and thoughts. Emotions are also commonly called "feelings," possibly because of the important role the physical sensations play in our ability to attach meaning to these complex "derived feelings." (43–45)

feedback: see "rapport." (74)

filters: see "constraints." (20)

4-tuple (4-T): one moment in time including the four parameters of visual, kinesthetic, auditory, and olfactory–gustatory experiences. Written as <V K A O>. (27)

generalization: the universal human modeling process of drawing from one or one set of experiences to understand and make predictions about similar new experiences. (9)

identification: this is a Meta Model violation in which the speaker has adopted a label as an accurate representation of reality. "I'm such an *idiot*" and "He's *crazy*" are two examples of this delusional thinking. (130–131)

individual constraints: the collection of our past personal history – our complete set of stored and remembered experiences – through which we filter our ongoing experiences. (27–31)

information retrieval behaviors: movements and gestures which are symptomatic of cerebral processes associated with retrieving stored (remembered) information. These include eye movements (146–152), breathing patterns (152–154), and body posturing (154).

internally generated stimuli: experiences <V K A O> which are drawn from memory. This "synthetic experience" can include any or all parameters of the 4-T and replaces at the moment in time it is being accessed the associated external experience in the 4-T. (27–29)

lead system: the system a person uses when he first starts to access internally stored information. The lead system is not always the same system as a person's preferred system. (48)

logical typing errors: mistaking the "map" for the "territory" it represents. Assuming that what you perceive (which is based on your own model of the world) is *reality*, and that it is the same as what other people perceive. (18–19)

lost performative: a Meta Model violation in which a person makes a value judgment or expresses a belief in a way that deletes the judge or the originator of the belief. (116–118)

mapping: a process by which you can determine a person's accessing cues schematic, his preferred representational system, and his representational system hierarchy. (155–162)

Meta Model: a linguistic tool for using portions of a person's spoken or written behavior to determine where he has generalized, deleted, or distorted experiences in his model of the world. It includes specific "Meta Model responses" to these "Meta Model violations" which aid in obtaining a more complete representation from the person's deep structure. Certain responses also help to reconnect the speaker with his deep structure in ways which can expand his perceptions and give him more choices about how to feel and behave. (77–80)

meta-perspective: an awareness of the *patterns* involved in the processes of communication as well as the content. (115)

metaphors: a speaker demonstrates this Meta Model violation when he uses metaphorical phrases as if they accurately reflect reality. "I keep getting into these *toxic* relationships. Maybe I'm the one who is *poisonous*!" is an example of this linguistic pattern. (135)

mind reading: a Meta Model violation in which a person expresses the idea that it is possible to know what someone else is thinking or feeling with little or no direct feedback. (108–110)

mirroring: see "rapport." (74)

modal operators: Meta Model violations which identify limits to a person's model of the world. Modal operators of necessity (102–103) are exemplified by imperatives such as "should," while modal operators of possibility (103–104) are exemplified by words such as "can't."

model: a representation of a thing or process which is useful as a tool for better understanding what it represents and for predicting how it will operate in various situations. A model is a generalized, deleted, and distorted copy of that which it represents. (5)

model of the world: a perceptual representation of our experiences of the world. A personal model of "reality," it differs from person to person depending on their neurological makeup and social and individual experiences. (3, 18)

multiordinality: this Meta Model violation occurs when a speaker uses ambiguous terms that can have different meanings in different contexts such as words like "love" or "relationship," especially when used in a way that indicates a probable barrier to achieving what he wants or an inability to avoid pain, as in, "It's just that love keeps getting in the way of my having a happy relationship." (125)

neurological constraints: the filters of our brain and sensory organs. Differences in people's "sensitivity" to various stimuli accounts in part for differences between people's models of the world. (20–23)

nominalization: a Meta Model violation in which an "abstract noun" is formed by taking a verb (such as "relate") and changing it by the process of linguistic distortion into a noun (like "relationship"). A nominalization differs from a "concrete noun" which names a person, place, or thing. (92–98)

nominalized: dissociated from kinesthetic aspects of experience through the use of language. A "digital" is often described as being "nominalized." (94, 97)

pacing: see "rapport." (74)

ocular accessing cues: eye accessing cues (EAC); see "accessing cues." (143–149)

over/under defined terms: a Meta Model violation in which the speaker confuses a word or phrase with reality, usually in the form of an evaluative expression like "good" or "counterproductive." (120–122)

perceptual enhancer: the effects of language on our perception. See also "social constraints." (78)

personalizing (Per.): when a speaker uses this Meta Model violation, he demonstrates a belief that someone's message or behavior (or even an event) that does not necessarily have anything to do with him is directed towards him personally. "The reason she's not here is because she's mad at me," could be true, but not *necessarily* true. "The only reason it rained was because we decided to camp out," is certainly not true.

predicate preference: the habitual use of certain predicates – verbs, adverbs, and adjectives – which indicate systematic use of one of the representational systems to express thoughts more often than the others. Predicate preference is often a good indication of a person's preferred representational system. (45)

preferred representation system (PRS): the system in which a person makes the most number of distinctions about himself and his environment. The habitual use of one system more often than the others to sort out and make sense of experiences demonstrates a person's PRS. (46)

pseudo words: these "false" descriptive words signal a Meta Model violation in which the speaker has completely "disconnected" from knowledge of or participation in the *processes* being used to create the description. Words such as "terrible" or "horrific," when used to describe an experience, not only effectively remove the speaker from any responsibility for that perception but also make it difficult to "see it from another point of view." (128–130)

pupil response: an unconscious response to emotional arousal. Directed by the autonomic nervous system, the pupils dilate when a person is exposed to pleasant stimuli and constrict when he is exposed to an unpleasant situation. (143–144)

rapport: during effective communication, rapport is established through communicative behaviors called "pacing." These subtle forms of feedback elicit in the observer a sense of *being like* and of *trusting* the communicator. Two methods of pacing that result in rapport are matching a person's predicate preference and "mirroring" (matching) a person's posture, gestures, rate of breathing, etc. (17–20, 74)

referential index: the person or thing doing or receiving the action of the verb in a sentence in the Meta Model, this is a violation where the person or thing has been *deleted* (85–86), *unspecified* (87–89), *generalized* (89–90), or *reversed* (90–92).

representational system hierarchy: the order of responsiveness to the world with the system in which a person makes the most number of distinctions (his preferred representational system) coming first and the least number of distinctions coming last. (55)

representational systems: literally referring to representations of experience (40), they include the visual system (46, 56–60), the kinesthetic system (47, 60–61), the auditory system (47, 62–63), the digital system (41, 63–64), and the olfactory system (47–48).

Satir categories: exaggerated postures and associated internal feelings about oneself. These include the "blamer," "placater," "computer," and "distracter." (70–72)

social constraints: cultural filters on our ability to perceive. Language, for example, can either enhance our perception of something by naming it ("perceptual enhancer"), or it can limit perception by not providing labels for certain aspects of experience. (23–25)

static words: these Meta Model violations occur when the speaker uses an abstract multiordinal nominalization as if it is the final verdict on an important aspect of ongoing experience. "I can't avoid the *insanity* of my job" is an example of this violation. (126)

stress: an important factor in determining how a person will respond in certain situations. Stress will often cause a person to "retreat" into the representational system in which he makes the most number of distinctions (his preferred system), thereby limiting both his awareness of the world and his choices about how to respond. (49–51)

subliminal cues: see "calibrated communication." (110)

surface structure (SS): the spoken or written portion of communication which is derived from the DS using the processes of generalization, deletion, and distortion. (81)

synthetic experience: see "internally generated stimuli." (27–29)

trust: within the context of effective communication, trust is the sense a person gets when he believes he is being understood. Trust is a necessary ingredient in the "magic" of effective communication and change. (17–20)

universal human modeling processes: three mechanisms common to all model-building activities – the processes of *generalization*, *deletion*, and *distortion*. (9–13)

universal quantifier: a Meta Model violation in which a generalization has been made in a way that indicates that the speaker is not aware of any exceptions to his statement, as with such words as "every" and "never." (105–108)

unspecified verbs: a Meta Model violation in which a person uses a verb which deletes such qualities as how, when, or where the activity took place or the duration or intensity of the act. (98–100)

Bibliography

Agus, D. B. *The End of Illness: A New Perspective on Health that Changes Everything*. New York: Simon & Schuster, 2012.

Bandler, R. and Grinder, J. *The Structure of Magic, Vol. I*. Palo Alto, CA: Science and Behavior Books, 1975.

Bandler, R. and Grinder, J. *The Structure of Magic, Vol. II*. Palo Alto, CA: Science and Behavior Books, 1976.

Bandler, R. and Grinder, J. *Frogs into Princes*. Moab, UT: Real People Press, 1979.

Bandler, R. and Grinder, J. and Satir, V. *Changing with Families*. Palo Alto, CA: Science and Behavior Books, 1976.

Bateson, G. *Steps to an Ecology of Mind*. New York: Ballantine Books, 1972.

Bogen, J. E. "Some educational aspects of hemispheric specialization." *U.C.L.A. Educator*, 17 (1975), 24–32.

Bois, J. S. *The Art of Awareness*, 3rd edn. Dubuque, IA: W.C. Brown Co., 1966.

Bostic St. Clair, C. and Grinder, J. *Whispering in the Wind*. Scotts Valley, CA: J and C Enterprises, 2001.

Brockman, J. (ed.) *About Bateson*. New York: E.P. Dutton, 1977.

Castaneda, C. *Tales of Power*. New York: Simon & Schuster, 1974.

Chomsky, N. *Language and Mind*, enlarged edn. New York: Harcourt Brace Jovanovich, 1972.

Coleman, J. C. *Abnormal Psychology and Modern Life*, 4th edn. Glenview, IL: Scott, Foresman and Co., 1972.

Darling, M. "A second look at NLP." *Training* (January 1988), pp. 38–42.

Diamantopoulos, G., Woolley, S., and Spann, M., "A critical review of past research into the neuro-linguistic programming of eye-accessing cues model," in P. Tosey (ed.), *Current Research in NLP*, Vol. 1: *Proceedings of the First International NLP Research Conference*. South Mimms, UK: ANLP International, 2009.

Dilts, R. "The NLP spelling strategy." Available at http://www.nlpu.com/Articles/artic10.htm (accessed February 28, 2012).

Dilts, R. and DeLozier, J. *The Encyclopedia of Systemic NLP and NLP New Coding*. Scotts Valley, CA: NLP University Press, 2000. Available at http://nlpuniversitypress.com (accessed February 24, 2012).

Edwards, B. *Drawing on the Right Side of the Brain*. New York: St. Martin's Press, 1979.

Ehrlichman, H., Micic, D., Sousa, A., and Zhu, J. "Looking for answers: eye movements in non-visual cognitive tasks," *Brain and Cognition*, 64:1 (2007), 7–20.

Einspruch, E. L. and Forman, B. D. "Observations concerning research literature on neuro-linguistic programming." *Journal of Counseling Psychology*, 32:4 (1985), 589–596.

Ellerbroek, W. "Language, emotion and disease." *Omni* 1:2 (1978), 93–120.

Ferguson, L. P. *Personality Development*. Belmont, CA: Wadsworth, 1970.

Frank, J. D. *Persuasion and Healing*. Baltimore, MD: Johns Hopkins University Press, 1973.

Friedman, K. "Learning the Arabs' silent language" (Edward T. Hall interview). *Psychology Today*, 13 (1979), 44–54.

Gibran, K. *The Prophet*. New York: Alfred A. Knopf, 1969.

Hall, E. T. *The Silent Language*. New York: Doubleday and Co., 1959.

Hall, E. T. *Beyond Culture*. New York: Anchor Press/Doubleday and Co., 1976.

Hall, L. M. *Communication Magic: Exploring the Structure and Meaning of Language*. Bancyfelin, Wales: Crown House Publishing, 2001.

Hall, L. M. *Meta States: Managing the Higher Levels of Your Mind's Reflexivity*, Clifton, CO: Neuro-Semantics Publications, 2002 [1995].

Heap, M. "Neurolinguistic programming – an interim verdict," in M. Heap (ed.), *Hypnosis: Current Clinical, Experimental and Forensic Practices*. London: Croom Helm, 1988, pp. 268–280.

Hess, E. *The Tell-Tale Eye*. New York: Van Nostrand Reinhold Co., 1975.

Hoag, J. D. "The NLP Meta Model." Available at http://www.nlpls.com/articles/NLPmetaModel.php (accessed February 28, 2012).

Huxley, A. *The Doors of Perception*. New York: Harper and Row, 1954.

Jung, C. G. *Man and His Symbols*. Garden City, NY: Doubleday, 1964.

Jung, C. G. *Collected Works of C.G. Jung*, Vol. 6: *Psychological Types*, ed. and trans. Gerhard Adler and R. F. C. Hull. Princeton, NJ: Princeton University Press, 1971 [1923].

Korzybski, A. *Science and Sanity: An Introduction to Non-Aristotelian Systems and General Semantics*, 5th edn. Chicago, IL: Institute of General Semantics, 1994.

Kroger, W. S. and Fezler, W. D. *Hypnosis and Behavior Modification: Imagery Conditioning*. Philadelphia, PA: J.B. Lippincott, 1976.

Lewis, B. *Sobriety Demystified: Getting Clean and Sober with NLP and CBT*. Santa Cruz, CA: Kelsey & Co., 1996.

Linder-Pelz, S. "Questions about meta-programs." *Acuity: Enhancing and Advancing Neuro Linguistic Programming*, 2 (2011), 78–91.

McClendon, T. *The Wild Days: NLP 1972–1981*. Cupertino, CA: Meta Publications, 1989.

Meichenbaum, D. *Cognitive Behavior Modification*. New York: Plenum Press, 1977.

Micic, D., Ehrlichman, H., and Chen, R. "Why do we move our eyes while trying to remember? The relationship between non-visual gaze patterns and memory." *Brain and Cognition*, 74:3 (2010), 210–224.

Morris, D. *Manwatching*. New York: Harry N. Abrams, 1977.

Palazzoli, M., Gianfranco, C., Giuiana, P., and Luigi, B. *Paradox and Counterparadox: A New Model in the Therapy of the Family in Schizophrenic Transaction*. New York: Jason Aronson, 1978.

Pullum, G. K. *The Great Eskimo Vocabulary Hoax and Other Irreverent Essays on the Study of Language*. Chicago, IL: University of Chicago Press, 1991.

Samuels, M. and Samuels, N. *Seeing with the Mind's Eye*. New York: Random House, 1975.

Satir, V. *Peoplemaking*. Palo Alto, CA: Science and Behavior Books, 1972.

Sharpley, C. F. "Predicate matching in NLP: a review of research on the preferred representational system." *Journal of Counseling Psychology*, 31:2 (1984), 238–248.

Sharpley, C. F. "Research findings on neurolinguistic programming: nonsupportive data or an untestable theory?" *Journal of Counseling Psychology*, 34:1 (1987), 103–107.

Sheldon, W. H. *The Varieties of Human Physique*. New York: Harper, 1940.

Sheldon, W. H. *The Varieties of Human Temperament*. New York: Harper, 1942.

Shepard, M. *Fritz*. New York: Bantam Books, 1975.

Shepard, R. *Visual Learning, Thinking and Communication*, ed. B. S. Randhawa and W. E. Coffman. New York: Academic Press, 1978.

Sperry, R. W., Gazzaniga, M. S., and Bogen, J. E. "Inter-hemispheric relationships: the neocortical commissures; syndromes of hemisphere disconnection," in P. J. Vinken and G. W. Bruyn (eds), *Handbook of Clinical Neurology*. Amsterdam: North-Holland Publishing, 1969, pp. 273–289.

Strupp, H. H., Fox, R. E., and Lessler, K. *Patients View Their Psychotherapy*. Baltimore, MD: Johns Hopkins University Press, 1969.

Tosey, P. and Mathison, J., "Fabulous creatures of HRD: a critical natural history of neuro-linguistic programming." Paper presented at the 8th International Conference on Human Resource Development, Research and Practice across Europe, Oxford, UK, June 26–28, 2007. Available at http://epubs.surrey.ac.uk/1193/1/fulltext.pdf (accessed February 24, 2012.)

Tosey, P. and Mathison, J. *Neuro-Linguistic Programming: A Critical Appreciation for Managers and Developers*. Basingstoke, UK: Macmillan, 2009.

Walsh, R. "Emerging cross-disciplinary parallels: suggestions from the neurosciences." *Journal of Transpersonal Psychology*, 11:2 (1979), 175–184.

Watzlawick, P., Beavin, J., and Jackson, D. *Pragmatics of Human Communication: A Study of Interactional Patterns, Pathologies, and Paradoxes*. New York: W.W. Norton, 1967.

Whorf, B. L. *Language, Thought, and Reality: Selected Writings of Benjamin Lee Whorf*, ed. J. B. Carol. New York: Wiley, 1956.

About the Author

At the time of this work's initial publication in 1980, Byron Lewis, M.A., was the director of the Meta Training Institute, a Northwest Educational and Consulting firm specializing in the techniques of Neuro-Linguistic Programming (NLP). As an undergraduate student at University of California, Santa Cruz in the mid-1970s, Byron studied under Dr. John Grinder and participated in the original research that laid the foundation for the now popular field of NLP.

Even before receiving his Masters in Psychology, Byron was actively involved in teaching communications seminars. A personable and entertaining seminar leader and consultant, Byron continued to conduct seminars and workshops in the field of NLP through 1985 when he moved to Germany. It was there that he began to work in the field of addictions, and during a career that spanned the next two decades, he published his second book, *Sobriety Demystified: Getting Clean and Sober with NLP and CBT* (1996) – now available from Crown House Publishing.